THE 20 MINUTE
VEGAN

THE 20 MINUTE VEGAN

QUICK, EASY FOOD

(that just so happens to be plant-based)

CALUM HARRIS

bluebird
books for life

CONTENTS

INTRODUCTION

IT'S ALL ABOUT ME.......8

THE PANTRY.......12

THE 20-MINUTE METHOD.......16

VEGAN COOKING TIPS & TRICKS.......17

THE TOOLS.......20

I'M THAT BATCH.......23

RECIPES

BRUNCH.......24

QUICK EATS.......54

PROPER EATS.......106

PUDS.......158

SNACKS 186

PICK-ME-UPS.......208

THE END BIT

WEEKLY PLANNERS.......222

INDEX.......230

THANK YOUS.......236

RECIPE INDEX

To help you decide what you fancy ... quickly

BRUNCH   24

Proper Porridge with a Cherry Jam   28
Fluffy Blueberry Pancakes   30
Fancy Apple & Cinnamon Oven Oats   34
Obviously Chocolatey Overnight Oats   37
Beaut Bircher   38
Peas on Toast   39
Tomato & Butter Bean Hummus on Toast   42
Boost-Me-Baby Bagel   44
Posh Beans on Toast   46
My Simple Tofu Scramble   48
One-pan Breakfast Veg Medley   51
Hearty Shakshuka   52

QUICK EATS   54

Creamy Harissa Chickpea Ciabattas   58
One-pot BBQ Mushroom Rice Bowl   60
Danny Danny Noodles   62
Boujee Black Bean & Quinoa Salad   65
Shredded Carrot Salad   66
The Go-to Greens Salad   68
Shredded Tofu Fajitas   70
'Chuna' Sandwich   73
Actually, A Decent Tomato Salad   74
Miso Me Up Stir-fry   76
Ready Red Pepper Pasta   78
Simply, A Noodle Soup   81
Spiced-up Fried Rice   82
Creamy Spinach Quesadillas   84
Quicker Nutty Ramen   86
Sunny Tomato Pesto Linguine   88
Green Goddess Soup   90
Thai-style Peanut Butter Curry   93
Garlicky Teriyaki Stir-fry   94
Tofu Shish Kebabs   98
Fiery Chilli Pasta   100
One-pot Messy Veg & Rice   102
Proper Peasto Pasta   104

MORNING PLAYLIST

SCAN ME

PROPER EATS 106

Sweet & Sticky Tofu	110
Creamy Chickpea Curry	112
A Kind-of Carbonara	114
Benny Bánh Mì	118
Butter 'Chicken' (Well Actually Tofu) Curry	120
Cherry Tomato Rigatoni	125
Smoky Barz Chilli	126
Jackfruit Chipotle Burritos	128
Tempeh Smash Burgers	130
The Ultimate Quick Bolognese	134
Mac & 'Cheese'	137
Miso Greens & Gnocchi	138
Bossman's Mushroom Kebabs	140
Cal's Tomato Soup	142
Pea & Mint Orzo	145
Tomatoey Chickpea & Broccoli Curry	146
Crispy Chilli Tofu	148
Hot Boy Summer Noodles	150
Tikka Tofu Wraps	152
The Salvador Dhali	155
Crispy Buffalo Tofu Tacos	156

EVENING PLAYLIST

SCAN ME

PUDS 158

Miso Banana Crumble	162
One-pan Cookie	164
Soft-baked Choc & Coffee Cookies	166
Salted Almond Butter Millionaires	168
Roasted Pistachio & Pineapple Medley	173
Mosconi's Tiramisu	174
Silky Chocolate Mousse	178
Cinnamony Crunch Flapjacks	180
Elite French Toast	183
Watermelon Sugar Shots	184

SNACKS & SIDES 186

Holy Harissa Hummus	190
Tempeh Nuggets	192
Spinach Satay Side	194
Sweet & Salty Tortilla Chips	197
Beaut Berry Granola Pots	198
Frozen Peanut Butter & Banana Bites	200
Carrot Cake Protein Balls	203
Blueberry Banoffee Smoothie	204
Ultimate Chocolate Smoothie	206
Get-Your-Greens-In Smoothie	207

PICK-ME-UPS 208

The Parmigiano Alternativo	212
Tahini Sauce	214
Jalapeño & Grape Salsa	217
Raita, My Way	218
Pico de Gallo con Corn	220

IT'S ALL ABOUT ME.

The introduction bit

Well, hello! Firstly, thanks for stopping by on this page. My name's Calum, and yes, this is a cookbook, my first cookbook (AHHH!), full of recipes that are not only fast, fresh and great for when you're absolutely starving, but also just happen to be vegan. Handy that, because, as you may have guessed, I am also vegan. To bring you up to speed with who I am and what this book is going to have in it, I'm writing an introduction. Let's go!

I started cooking back in 2015, not only because I wanted to eat more healthily, but also because cooking is a brilliant skill to have, and it bloody well impresses a lot of people. I started making my own dishes and did this for a few years, learning from my mum, cookbooks and people on the Internet.

My journey with food swerved in a different direction when I went to a barbecue in 2018. At this barbecue was a family friend, called Pan. As I went about my day, eating chicken, steak and salmon and everything you'd expect, he was eating his own food. And it looked decent. By the way, this guy was jacked, and looked pretty healthy too. I asked him, plain and simple, what he was eating, and that's when the penny dropped. He was vegan. No wonder his plate had colour on it. This was also at the time when I was curious about everything, so I asked him why he was plant-based. He shared great arguments for going vegan, whether from an environmental, ethical or health point of view. I thought, 'Do you know what, Mr Greek Man with the jacked physique: you've got a point.' I'm no preacher, and this isn't the book for me to get into all of the reasons in detail, however, in summary, the food system has arguably the biggest impact on the planet, and the people and animals living on it. Going vegan, or eating more vegan food, is clearly a healthier choice not only for us, but also for the planet (yes, that old saying). So, I tried it for a month, fully expecting I'd go back to eating meat, dairy and fish. And five years later, I'm here. Still kicking, still healthy, and enjoying the food I make. FIVE YEARS! WOAH. I can honestly say it does not feel like five years, it's genuinely flown by.

While I was starting to discover my plant-based persona, I began to notice that others were sharing their vegan recipes on social media. However, as much as they looked delicious and scrummy, they didn't give me what I wanted. I wanted meals that you could make on a regular basis, that had protein in them, that used ingredients I could easily buy from the supermarket, that didn't rely on heavily-processed meat and dairy alternatives, and above all, didn't take an hour or two to make. And so, in 2019, I started a social media page, making videos on just that. And in the space of four years, I've built a following online, and even got on TV. I'll explain how that came about, shall I? Around September 2021, I saw a post from Jamie Oliver looking for applications for his new show *The Great Cookbook Challenge* after being sent it by someone on my Instagram (I don't know who this was but thank you, because you changed my life). I applied, not thinking I'd get picked, and then a week later, I had to drop everything to film the first episode in a few weeks' time. The show's aim was to take eighteen home cooks and set various challenges, with the winner being awarded their own cookbook deal. I can't lie, I wasn't thinking about if I was going to win or not, in fact I was more concerned with the elephant in the room: meeting Jamie Oliver. Jamie is a hero of mine, and I was so nervous to meet him, let alone cook in front of him.

I was a chattering, blubbering mess in that first episode, even having the cheek to call him my dad (Jamie's first book *The Naked Chef* being released in 1999, the same year I was born, so yes, him being my dad is plausible). But somehow, I got through it, and even got into the final five of the show. All of this, and hundreds of tried-and-tested recipes later, I'm here writing this. In my cookbook. The debut. The first one. Of many? I don't know, I hope. Let's all hope.

That's me, to a tee. I'm not a chef, nor will I ever call myself one. I'm a self-taught cook, who made loads of videos, and all in all, wants more people to make more vegan food. Now, naturally, you're thinking, this book is 'a bit of me', but …

Why 20 minutes, and why another vegan cookbook?

It's simple. Everyone is focused on their lives right now, in a time when we don't know what is going on or what life will bring. Our priorities deep down are friends, partners, family and work. And in this routine, cooking gets put on a backburner, especially if you're making vegan food. And I get it. If I was working a 9–5 with continuous brain activity, maybe followed by a spin class or a cheeky pint with work, then came back after a commute and you told me I should cook a vegan meal that I'd never made before and that it would take an hour to do it, I'd order a takeaway and then go to bed. I know vegan cooking can be quick, easy and delicious, so why doesn't anyone tell us that? I actually don't know. So let me show you how to do it.

And the next question, why another vegan cookbook, specifically, why this one? I believe that with these recipes in the book, and a couple of adjustments to your weekly shop, you'll be absolutely flying and eating more vegan food in no time – and you'll actually stick with it. You'll also realise that it's easier than you think. You only need a little bit of prep to make healthy meals from scratch that look like the rainbow and taste gorgeous. As well as this, portion sizes are generous in this book, because let's face it, I don't want you to finish a meal still starving, and you deserve a good amount of food.

Nutritional info

Should you need it, every recipe has nutritional information checked off by a brilliant dietitian. In fact, here's a quote from her:

Eating healthily as a vegan is not about one particular meal or nutrient, but the overall balance and variety of what we eat over time. Most of the recipes in Calum's book provide you with a good source of plant-based protein and other important nutrients, and there are also some lovely treats to enjoy every now and then as part of your balanced meals.

CLARE GRAY, REGISTERED SPECIALIST DIETITIAN

MYTH-BUSTING

1 —→ Where's your protein?

Believe it or not, vegan meals have protein in them, you don't need the meat to pack it with protein, just being honest. I've made sure that the meals in this book *are* packed with protein, but the priority for me was making the meals satisfying, and filling, rather than trying to overdo it on the protein side of things. You've got variety, too (it's not a tofu-only cookbook, don't worry), including beautiful recipes with chickpeas, peas, lentils, grains and a smidge of protein powder here and there.

2 —→ Why does it take so long to cook vegan food?

Well, nah, it doesn't. The majority of the dishes in this book are prepped and cooked in 20 minutes or less. There are just a few brilliant recipes in the book that require a bit more time.

3 —→ Vegan cooking is expensive!

I don't want to break the bank for you, babe! And I agree, it's not as if we're dating or anything. Most of the vegan products that are considered expensive are like-for-like alternatives. I don't believe you need them at all, so I've done my best to include absolutely none of them in this book. Yes, you'll be buying ingredients for your pantry that are new to you and yes, that'll be the pricey shop that week. However, everything there you'll end up using all the time, and repeatedly come up in recipes in this book!

4 —→ Vegan food is boring

Like I'd rather play chess and watch my neighbour Susan put up her fencing. I wear big white glasses and vegan pearls when I'm out, do I look like I do boring food? I do believe vegan cooking is fun, to the point where I get joy from cracking a joke in each recipe. If you find this difficult at first, at least you'll have a laugh reading them. Flavour is also a recurring guest in all the recipes here, like genuinely, you'll be surprised with how good some of these dishes are.

5 —→ This book just uses vegan cheese, vegan chicken and vegan knockoffs of the real thing I bet?

No again. The book uses ingredients you're able to grab in your supermarket. There are only three vegan alternatives: oat or soy milk, vegan yogurt and a vegan cheese slice for your burger if you want it. The rest of the book uses ingredients with minimal processing.

THE PANTRY: THE OLD ESSENTIALS ON THE BLOCK

So, next point of action; what do you need to buy? Read the recipes, come on, don't be lazy. I'm kidding. I've popped a list of old things you know, and new things you'll need.

PEANUT BUTTER

Nut butters taste creamy, are rich in good fats, and I don't think I can have a life without peanut butter in my kitchen.

BALSAMIC VINEGAR

We all dip our bread in it, but this is great for dressings, topping pasta and adding a nice acidity kick to recipes such as the Bolognese.

COCONUT CREAM
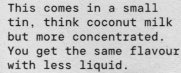

This comes in a small tin, think coconut milk but more concentrated. You get the same flavour with less liquid.

ALMOND BUTTER

I make sure to choose nut butters that only include the nuts and a pinch of salt in the ingredients.

SOY SAUCE

Perfection in a bottle, soy sauce gives a great umami taste. Light has less salt, dark is richer and gives a nice colour to dishes - both work in their own way depending on the recipe.

GOOD FLAKY SALT + PEPPER

Seasoning is key for cooking, especially vegan recipes. So please, taste food as you go along and adjust to your liking.

OLIVE OILS

I use light olive oil for frying and extra virgin olive oil for dressings and for roasting.

SPICES

From top to bottom: smoked paprika, cumin, cinnamon and garam masala are my go-to dried spices in the book.

TOMATO PASTE

This is the perfect little number to get that tomatoey goodness in dishes.

DRIED HERBS

You can't go wrong with dried mixed herbs — they pack a big flavour punch.

THE PANTRY: THE NEW ESSENTIALS ON THE BLOCK

TAHINI

This is a sesame seed paste perfect for dressings, hummus and drizzling on top of dishes.

MAPLE SYRUP

Bye-bye honey, hello two newbies: maple and agave. I like both; maple is richer in flavour.

MIRIN

A sweet rice wine vinegar that I use a lot in the Asian-style recipes in this book.

GOCHUJANG

Smoky, spicy and sort of sweet, this one's a go-to of mine if I fancy some spice in my life.

SILKEN TOFU

It's low fat, high protein and a better alternative for dairy-free cream. The ones I go for are Clearspring or J-Basket.

APPLE CIDER VINEGAR

Vinegar is a great mate to have in your cooking artillery, and perfect for acidity in dishes, which sounds science-y but it just means it adds a sourness. Apple cider is my favourite variety.

ROSE HARISSA

A smoky but sort of floral flavour. That won't make sense, but harissa is so unique in flavour you need it in your life.

NUTRITIONAL YEAST

Essentially, if you want your dishes to taste like they've got Parmesan in them, this is the one. I prefer Marigold.

AGAVE SYRUP

Another option for honey, agave is cheaper than maple, but pick your favourite.

MISO PASTE

A flavourbomb. It has got such a great umami taste, and where we lack in meat, we make up for in flavour with this. I like the Miso Tasty one.

THE 20-MINUTE METHOD

Tips and tricks to get the recipes done and to cook better really.

Let me help you out by getting your cooking game up. Firstly, 20 minutes for me means 15 minutes with room for a little chat or to find an ingredient that's at the back of the fridge. I don't have a stopwatch while I'm cooking, as that would be too strict and I'd have no social life. All these recipes have been tested by me and others and timed to the minute. I wanted to share some tricks to not only get these recipes done in quick time, but also improve your cooking game for not just these recipes but others. Here's my method that I've popped into five steps or tips or whatever you fancy calling them.

⟶ Don't rush
Defeats the point of the book, doesn't it? Well, not exactly. I want people to see how easy vegan cooking can be. Now for people who are confident cooks, they'll breeze through it, but what if you've never cooked before in your life and this is the first meal you make? Let alone a vegan one. Work with your skillset, read each step before beginning to get the right equipment out and fall in love with the process of cooking. Then as you get into it, you'll get quicker and more experienced. By the end, you'll be giving me a handshake for turning you into a proper home cook, like a Marvel hero, but for cooking.

⟶ Organise your ingredients
You might already be doing this, but if not, this will be a massive help. To cook more efficiently, I put the ingredients I'm using in the recipe next to where I'm going to be using them. So, for example, all the veg will go by the chopping board, the spices and sauces will go right by my oven hob and the bits to finish will go on the table.

⟶ Prepare and plan
This is an easy step, but wash your veggies and measure bits out where required. Most of the cooking in here you figure out by tasting as you go, but in other recipes, there are occasions where every measurement matters and you have to make sure you measure exactly. I'm not naming any names, but it's BAKING.

⟶ Stick some music on
Cooking is boring, right? Wrong. Make it fun, isn't there a new Frank Ocean album out to listen to? Probably not, but let's hope it is by the time this book is out. I have some Spotify playlists (see pages 6–7) that I cook to depending on my mood, and trust me it's a shift change. I can go from Nas to Ludovico Einaudi to Fred Again.. on different days, so make sure to check them out depending on what you like.

⟶ Have fun with it
That's all I can ask really. My recipes are meant for everyday cooking, so have fun being with me every single day, potentially. So enjoy it, enjoy this book, and thank you in advance for using it to cook from.

VEGAN COOKING TIPS & TRICKS

These are essentially quick tips of mine for general cooking, and will hopefully help you to cook from all the books you read, not just mine - but I'd love it to be mine.

1 ⟶ Umami and papi

Soy sauce, miso paste, shiitake mushrooms – these ingredients each have their own flavour that I cannot describe, but they're so distinct that you must use them. And eventually, like a mum and dad, your skills as the papi of the kitchen will be celebrated due to your umami flavour (get it? Great).

2 ⟶ Salt and pepper are not just a hip-hop duo but your best mates

Seasoning food is without a doubt the most important thing to do during cooking. I salt and pepper in three stages; after adding the base ingredients (onions, carrots, garlic, etc), after doing most of the recipe, and one final season at the end of cooking. Works every time.

3 ⟶ Just a little bit

This is the sweet tip. Apart from the desserts, of course, some dishes can benefit from a surprise hit of sweetness. The most common one being agave or maple syrup in savoury dishes but sometimes a square of chocolate in rich dishes. Why not add an extra square of dark chocolate to the Smoky Barz Chilli (see page 126)? See what happens.

4 ⟶ Acid creates a party in your mouth

Not the types you get in a warehouse, but the types that elevate dishes and give it a zing, or a freshness. That's why you might find a lemon, some apple cider vinegar, or a little lime juice make their way into dishes you won't expect. You'll be surprised how much a small squeeze makes a difference.

5 ⟶ My cooking has no rules

Ironic isn't it as I've just given some tips which can be read like rules. But my point? Cooking is an art, and like art, everything is up for discussion, there's no right way to make a dish, especially a vegan one. You might see some recipes here and go 'I could do this better' or 'this could do with a bit of Tabasco', but that's the point. We've all got different palates and tastes, so use them! Because there's no tradition in vegan cooking, especially mine, so change it up if you fancy it.

IT'S ALL PLANT-BASED. ALL UNDER 20 MINUTES. SOMEHOW.

THE TOOLS

I don't like gadgety or one-use appliances, and for me, my cooking set up has not changed over the years that I've been cooking. I don't see this changing either. So in this book, on my socials, and in hopefully more recipes to come, this equipment list won't change, and will be the perfect base to get you properly on the way with cooking my recipes. And there's no air fryer, sorry not sorry.

⟶ **Food processor**
A large one will take you to the moon and back. I use it to make a lot of sauces for pasta, soups, smoothies, desserts, and also when I can't be bothered to chop up.

⟶ **Good knives**
A 6-inch chef's knife, a cleaver or a Santoku knife and a bread knife. These are the three I end up using. Go out to a shop or have a google and you should be able to find them.

⟶ **Chopping board**
A wooden one is great.

⟶ **Large (and slightly deep) frying pan**
Mine is 28cm to be exact, but I use this pan for nearly all my cooking. If it's ovenproof, that's a nice bonus.

⟶ **Large and small saucepans**
Both great, the difference? The little one you might use for when you can't be bothered to get the big one out.

⟶ **Box grater**
This is grate (see what I did there) for breaking down garlic, ginger, carrots and other veg, instead of chopping it finely.

⟶ **Oven**
It goes without saying but get ready to use it.

⟶ **Roasting tray**
Basically the thing you shove everything on in the oven. Thin one, about 40cm in length.

⟶ **Silicone spatula**
Ideally hold it better than I do (I've been ridiculed for holding a spatula oddly online).

⟶ **Microplane**
This is an extra flair. But it is great to get zesting done, and maybe if you want to have really, really fine garlic. You can warm up to this one, and use a box grater instead.

⟶ **Toaster**
You should have it, but it toasts, you guessed it, bread.

⟶ **Kettle**
I don't know why, but something tells me that I should tell people to buy a kettle. If they don't already have one.

⟶ **Microwave**
'Ohhh a microwave is bad for you.' It's not. It's not. Use it, it's great for when you need to cook rice in a hurry or quickly heat things up.

I'M THAT BATCH

This is a 20-minute vegan cookbook, as you might've gathered from the title, but there's no doubt in my mind that you'll want to make dishes in advance, or you'll make more than what you need. So here's my little indicators about what you can probably make in advance, and what you can batch up.

⟶ **Most of the mains serve 2–3 people.** This is a generous portion for two people or a lighter portion for three people. So just a simple double up and you get great portions to feed a family of four. Always read the recipe before you shop as some recipes already serve more than 2–3 people.

⟶ **Desserts can serve a group of four people.** Except the mousse. So make them for a Friday night in or to serve a dinner party.

⟶ **The night before** you can prep the two overnight oat recipes, and I highly recommend doing that on a Sunday to begin Monday with a bang.

⟶ **All the pasta sauces can be made in advance** – and they'll keep in the fridge for a good 3–5 days in an airtight container, so you can have great pasta sauces at your disposal whenever you fancy it. Just use some pasta water to make them properly saucy when you mix them with pasta.

⟶ **Make the Pick-Me-Ups before you make any of the meals.** It allows you to not only have them ready when the food is, but I find it nice when you get the side dishes done first, before you tackle the main.

⟶ **Soups for all** – again, airtight container, make the soup the night before and bring to work for the next day.

⟶ **The curries and chillies are beautifully batchy** – I don't know what that means but make them in advance, the flavours mingle in the fridge, and you end up with a bold lunch for the next day, or freeze in an airtight container for up to a month.

⟶ **Double up the sandwich recipes and serve to more people** – for example, the 'Chuna' Sandwich and the Creamy Harissa Chickpea Ciabattas are great for this. You can also double the Crispy Buffalo Tofu Tacos to serve a board full of tacos to a good party of four. I'd recommend making the salsas from Pick-Me-Ups on the same day to enjoy with them.

BRUNCH

1

IS IT LUNCH OR IS IT BREAKFAST?

Either way, this is the chapter with recipes that are breakfast-y.

All I know is that these dishes are meant to be enjoyed in the morning.

Whether you need a fast nutritious hit or something energy-boosting to save your weekend, there'll no doubt be something here that gives you an oomph to begin your day.

There are two types of recipes for breakfast: the ones you can eat in a rush and the ones you would probably eat on a weekend. All the recipes here make beautiful breakfasts for you and someone else. But like a parent when they say they 'haven't got a favourite', I do. The Hearty Shakshuka (see page 52) and the Fluffy Blueberry Pancakes (page 30) are to die for.

PROPER PORRIDGE WITH A CHERRY JAM

Your go-to oat recipe, with a fruity facelift.

Oats in the morning is a must for some, but might not be for all. Which is why I want to get you back into it, and there's no better way than actually giving your breakfast some love (stop it). I make mine nice with a fruity jam or, as the posh restaurants call it, a compote. This is my go-to porridge recipe that you'll end up falling for, and using frozen berries makes this one you can have all year round.

*3 mins prep + 12 mins cooking = **15 mins total***

MAKES 2 NICE BOWLS

80g porridge oats
300ml oat (or soy) milk
1 scoop (30g) vegan vanilla
 protein powder (optional)
1 tbsp agave syrup
handful of pecans (about 20g)
cacao nibs, to garnish
hemp seeds, to garnish
 (optional)

For the cherry jam
100g frozen cherries
10ml (tiny splash of) hot water
2 tbsp agave syrup
juice of ½ lemon

TOP TIP:

You can have porridge however thick or thin as you like. I like it thick – if you took a tablespoon of the good stuff and turned the spoon upside down, it would stay stuck to the spoon but close to falling off.

1. Put the oats in a small saucepan on a medium heat and toast for 1 minute – with no oil, just in case you dared to think, 'ah I must have it'.

2. Next, add the oat milk and protein powder (if using) to the saucepan, stir it up and, once it's hot – like British hot – turn the heat down to low and let the oats simmer for a good 8 minutes or so. If it gets thick quickly, add a splash more of milk or water to help loosen up the porridge.

3. At the same time, chuck the cherries in another small saucepan or frying pan, as well as the hot water, agave syrup and lemon juice. Let it bubble away on a medium heat and keep stirring for 8–10 minutes until the cherries defrost and the mixture goes all jammy.

4. Once the oats are thick, like gripping-a-tablespoon thick, add a little extra splash of oat milk, then the agave syrup. Once thick, turn off the heat.

5. Bash up the pecans using a pestle and mortar, a quick pulse in the food processor, or even just your knife, and get that ready for the end.

6. Serve up your porridge in bowls (not sure what else you'd serve it in to be honest) and top it with the cherry jam, then a pinch of bashed-up pecans and, finally, cacao nibs. You can also add hemp seeds if you can get your hands on them, as they're a real superfood.

CALS: 519 | **PROTEIN:** 20g | **FAT:** 20g | **SAT FAT:** 3.9g | **CARBS:** 61g | **SUGAR:** 29g | **SALT:** 0.63g | **FIBRE:** 9.5g

FLUFFY BLUEBERRY PANCAKES

The only way you should be making pancakes.

Let me settle the debate here: pancakes are not crêpes. And crêpes are not pancakes. There is a discussion that people prefer crêpes over pancakes, which is fine, you do you. But I think nothing beats a fat stack of pancakes, and the proper way. Team America. They're best served with this easy blueberry jam, or compote if you talk fancy. I'd say this makes enough for 3–4 people.

*12 mins prep + 8 mins cooking = **20 mins total***

MAKES 8–10 MEDIUM-SIZED PANCAKES OR 4–5 FAT ONES

For the batter
2 ripe bananas
140g self-raising flour
30g vegan vanilla protein powder
1 tsp baking powder
pinch of salt
1 tsp agave or maple syrup
250ml plant milk (oat or soy works best)
1 tbsp flaxseed
coconut or light olive oil, for frying
vegan butter, to serve (optional)

For the blueberry jam
100g (bowlful of) frozen blueberries
20ml hot water
2 tbsp agave or maple syrup
2 tbsp desiccated coconut
juice of ½ lemon

1. Let's make the batter. In a large bowl, mash the bananas until smooth and not lumpy whatsoever, then mix the dry and wet ingredients together. Let that batter sit for 8 minutes before frying. The reason? Flaxseed helps bind everything together, quite like an egg would, and it takes a little moment to kick in, so give it that time please.

2. Meanwhile, blueberry jam? Yes lad. Combine the blueberries, water, syrup, desiccated coconut and lemon juice in a small saucepan on a medium heat. Cook for 5–7 minutes or until the blueberries have fully blistered and the mixture has gone sweet, thick and juicy – cheeky. It should still have a little liquid. If it reduces too much, add a splash more hot water.

3. Heat about a teaspoon of oil in a large frying pan on a medium heat and make sure the entire base of the pan is covered. No gaps please. Right now, the fun bit. Spoon 2–3 tablespoons of batter per pancake and cook for 1–2 minutes on each side, or until you see bubbles covering the edges of the pancake. You should be able to cook 2–3 pancakes per go. Once flipped, press them down gently to squeeze the batter out, making sure it all gets cooked. Repeat with the rest of the batter. You will also have to reapply oil when cooking further batches, just so you know and don't moan at me for your pancakes sticking.

4. Serve your pancakes stacked up as high as you'd like. Dollop the blueberry jam over the top and garnish with more desiccated coconut and maybe dollops of vegan butter and more agave (because why not?). Enjoy, devour, and show off with your pancakes.

CALS: 364 | **PROTEIN:** 10g | **FAT:** 13g | **SAT FAT:** 8.5g | **CARBS:** 48g | **SUGAR:** 18g | **SALT:** 1g | **FIBRE:** 6g

Making
stacks

No I'm not wearing
a tablecloth

FANCY APPLE & CINNAMON OVEN OATS

I'm sorry, what?

This one's a winner. In all honesty I've probably said this for more than ten of the recipes in here, but this one's different. There's a real magic in this - it's essentially having cake for breakfast. Somehow, it also reminds me of my nan. I'll explain, don't worry. One of the first things I cooked, or baked actually, was an apple pie with my nan. She would use Granny Smiths, shop-bought pastry and tons of sugar. And now, 20 years later, I'm returning the favour to her with this recipe.

*5 mins prep + 15 mins cooking = **20 mins total***

SERVES 2

½ banana
100g porridge oats
30g vegan vanilla protein powder (or 1 tsp vanilla extract)
250ml plant milk (oat or soy works best)
1 tsp baking powder
pinch of salt
1 tsp ground cinnamon
1 Pink Lady apple
2 tbsp agave or maple syrup

1. Preheat the oven to 200°C (fan 180°C/gas mark 6).

2. Mash the banana with a fork in a small baking dish until there are no lumps, then add the oats, protein powder or vanilla extract, milk, baking powder, salt and cinnamon. Mix until everything's all combined and the oats are looking a bit like overnight oats.

3. Slice your apple into quarters, cutting around the core. Slice thinly across each quarter until you have beautiful little slices of apple. Arrange them on top of the oats like petals on a flower or in a spiral, making sure there's no overlap, until you've used all the apple slices or you've run out of room.

4. Drizzle the agave or maple syrup over the top of the apples and bake it for 15 minutes.

5. Eat it up, when it's warm. Not straight out the oven, you dingbat. Was that uncalled for? Probably, but yeah, enjoy the beauty of eating cake for breakfast.

CALS: 432 | **PROTEIN:** 18g | **FAT:** 8.5g | **SAT FAT:** 1.3g | **CARBS:** 67g | **SUGAR:** 29g | **SALT:** 1.4g | **FIBRE:** 9.2g

OBVIOUSLY CHOCOLATEY OVERNIGHT OATS

I know what you're thinking. 'Why am I making a breakfast recipe when it's dinner time?' And it's because I believe, like those people who are into trading (couldn't be me, I just cook great food), putting in the work early is a great return on investment for later on. And this chocolatey oaty recipe deserves your love and attention in the evening before you wake up to it in the morning!

*2 mins prep + 3 mins making + time in the fridge overnight = **5 mins and a good sleep***

SERVES 2

2 squares of 70% dark chocolate
80g jumbo oats
2 tbsp cacao powder
1 scoop (30g) vanilla vegan protein powder (optional)
300ml plant milk (oat or soy works best)
1 tsp agave syrup
1 tbsp hemp seeds
30g fresh raspberries
1 tbsp cacao nibs

1. Cut the dark chocolate squares into small chunks, then combine all the ingredients except the raspberries and cacao nibs in a container that has a lid. It should look like your oats are swimming in a bath and they've got loads of room to move. That's fine, mate, don't add more oats.

2. Pop a lid on the top and leave in the fridge overnight for the oats to soak.

3. Grab the oats out of the fridge the next morning, and in a surprise turn of events that's not that surprising to me, the oats are lusciously smooth and all ready to be devoured by you.

4. Before you get the oats out of the fridge, get the raspberries in a small bowl and mash lightly with a spoon.

5. Pour the oats into a serving bowl or eat it out of the container at this point, topping it with the freshly mashed raspberries and cacao nibs.

6. Go to work, or stay at home, or go to work, or stay at home ... either way, enjoy the day.

The prepped breakfast you deserve in your life.

CALS: 440 | **PROTEIN:** 24g | **FAT:** 20g | **SAT FAT:** 7.3g | **CARBS:** 36g | **SUGAR:** 4.8g | **SALT:** 0.63g | **FIBRE:** 11g

BEAUT BIRCHER

Bircher mueslis are brilliant. They're essentially the OG overnight oats, before overnight oats went big time. And they're lovely. Made in Switzerland, and now in a British bloke's book, you'll be making this all year round. It's packed with oats and fruit, and has this perfect balance of creaminess and freshness. What more could you want? Apart from me making it for you …

*5 mins prep + a night in the fridge = **8 mins before you go to bed***

SERVES 2

1½ red apples
20g pecans, plus extra for topping
80g porridge or jumbo oats
1 tsp ground cinnamon
20g (little handful) sultanas, plus a few extra for topping
20g (little handful) raisins
1 scoop (30g) vanilla vegan protein powder (optional)
1 tbsp agave syrup (to taste)
250ml plant milk (oat or soy works best)
2 tbsp vegan Greek-style yogurt

1. Grate 1 apple using a box grater, that's it. Then crumble up the pecans with your hands and put that and the apple into a container that has a lid. That's all you need to do for step 1.

2. Pop all the other ingredients into that container, but add the milk and yogurt last of all. Stir to combine everything together. You should have oats swimming in the milk, and that's okay!

3. Pop a lid on the top and leave in the fridge overnight.

4. Open the fridge in the morning, top with pecans, some slices of apple, pinch of sultanas, and like a kid on Christmas Day, be amazed at what's turned up. Tuck in.

I can see why people go on about muesli now.

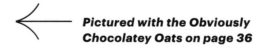

← ***Pictured with the Obviously Chocolatey Oats on page 36***

CALS: 523 | **PROTEIN:** 21g | **FAT:** 16g | **SAT FAT:** 2g | **CARBS:** 68g | **SUGAR:** 38g | **SALT:** 0.79g | **FIBRE:** 11g

PEAS ON TOAST

Basically avocado on toast's better-looking cousin.

Don't even give me that 'no, no, this is not it' chat. As an avocado lover myself, I can confirm this absolutely works, and holds its weight among the other toppings on toast. It's fresh, creamy, and I guarantee you'll keep a pack of peas in the freezer to repeat this.

*5 mins prep + 5 mins cook = **10 mins total***

SERVES 2

100g frozen peas
1 garlic clove
2 tbsp runny tahini
pinch of fresh parsley
juice of 1 lime, plus extra to serve
1 tbsp extra virgin olive oil
2 slices of sourdough bread
salt and pepper
pinch of dried chilli flakes, to serve (optional)

1. Defrost the peas. This only takes a minute or two, but I recommend putting them into a heatproof bowl, covering them in boiling water and letting them defrost that way.

2. Drain the peas, then remove the garlic clove from its skin by bashing it with the flat side of the knife. Put the peas, the bashed garlic clove and the rest of the ingredients (minus the bread and chilli) in a food processor and blitz till smooth. It should actually resemble mashed avocado.

3. Toast your bread then serve it all up. Add a pinch of chilli flakes on top if you fancy it, and maybe an extra squeeze of lime.

Pictured overleaf

CALS: 432 | **PROTEIN:** 16g | **FAT:** 19g | **SAT FAT:** 2.9g | **CARBS:** 46g | **SUGAR:** 5g | **SALT:** 1.6g | **FIBRE:** 6.2g

Avocado? Nah mate,
move out the way.

TOMATO & BUTTER BEAN HUMMUS ON TOAST

I can't lie, I don't do what I call 'posh breakfasts'. These are what I like to call 'breakfasts that you wouldn't do if you were rushing out the house but if you had some time on a weekend, do it then'. However, this breakfast in particular has to be a must for you all. The juicy tomatoes work so well with the creamy butter bean hummus, and honestly, it bangs.

*5 mins prep + 15 mins cooking = **20 mins total***

SERVES 2

250g cherry vine tomatoes
baking paper (not an ingredient
    but something you may have
    to go to the shops and get)
3 tbsp extra virgin olive oil,
    plus extra for drizzling
1 x 400g tin butter beans
2 garlic cloves
4 tbsp tahini
juice of 1½ lemons
1 tsp ground cumin
100ml ice-cold water
salt and pepper

To serve
2 slices sourdough bread
1 tsp rose harissa
juice of ½ lemon
handful of wild rocket

TOP TIP:

Instead of roasting, you can pan-fry the tomatoes in a large frying pan with olive oil until they have softened and blistered, but don't leak all their juices.

1. Oven, do you have one? Great. Shove it on at 200°C (fan 180°C/gas mark 6).

2. Remove the vines from the cherry tomatoes and pop those tomatoes in a roasting tray lined with baking paper. Add a pinch each of salt and pepper, drizzle with extra virgin olive oil and roast for 15 minutes if you would be so kind.

3. Hummus time. Drain the butter beans using a colander and add to a food processor with all the remaining ingredients except the water. Blitz to form a smooth but thick paste, then gradually add the water until you have a light but firm hummus. You'll know when it's ready, as it will look like, well, hummus. You will have to season to taste with salt and lemon, and you might not have to add all the 100ml of water, so this is when you're gonna be a proper chef and do your best!

4. Now toast the sourdough. Please. Done it? Pop it on a plate and drizzle with a tiny bit of extra virgin olive oil. Then use a spoon to dollop on the hummus. Make room on the top for the tomatoes and add them on top of that gorgeous hummus.

5. Finish the toast with a drizzle of rose harissa, a tiny squeeze of lemon juice and some rocket leaves.

6. Take this opportunity to take a photo, send it to a relative, show them what you created, and eat it. Also, don't forget to turn off the oven.

CALS: 772 | **PROTEIN:** 23g | **FAT:** 45g | **SAT FAT:** 6.6g | **CARBS:** 61g | **SUGAR:** 8.5g | **SALT:** 1.3g | **FIBRE:** 11g

BOOST-ME-BABY BAGEL

I absolutely love bagels, but I definitely do not have them enough. But one thing I did love, when I used to eat meat, was a bacon (I know, sorry) sandwich. It was the ultimate saviour the morning after a night of age-appropriate drinking. Which is why I decided, when I became vegan, that I wanted to fill that void and make something moreish, but also not too greasy to make me feel bad about myself after scoffing it down in 2 minutes flat. So, if you're reading this at 10:44am and you're craving something fulfilling, then I've got you sorted.

*8 mins prep + 10 mins cooking = **18 mins total***

SERVES 2

100g cherry tomatoes
4 tbsp light olive oil
1 tbsp tomato paste
2 garlic cloves
1 x 200g block of tempeh
1 tbsp agave syrup (plus 1 tbsp for the tomato ketchup, optional)
4 tbsp light soy sauce
1 tsp sweet smoked paprika
2 wholemeal or white bagels
vegan butter, for spreading, or extra virgin olive oil, for drizzling
handful of wild rocket
salt and pepper

TOP TIP:

If you have a cylinder block of tempeh, stand it up tall and chop the outer slices until you make a cuboid. It's then much easier to slice.

1. Right. First off, prick the cherry tomatoes with a knife and pop them in a small saucepan with 1 tablespoon of the olive oil on a medium heat. Let the tomatoes burst, then add the tomato paste. Please also peel the garlic cloves and put them into the saucepan whole. What we're doing here is making a makeshift, chunky ketchup.

2. Cut the block of tempeh into long, thin slices. Pop them into a large frying pan with the remaining olive oil on a medium heat and fry for 3 minutes each side until golden.

3. Keep an eye on the tomatoes and garlic and make sure they do not burn. Keep cooking until the tomatoes are barely visible and you're left with a chunky tomato sauce. Fish out the garlic cloves with a tablespoon, then season to taste with salt and pepper and a tablespoon of agave syrup if you fancy making it slightly sweeter.

4. Once you've toasted one side of the tempeh, and it's golden just like track 1 of the *Fine Line* album, add the soy sauce, paprika and a tablespoon of agave syrup and toss it all together until the rashers are coated, and look somewhat 'bacony'. That's not a real adjective but I bet it makes sense when you're cooking it.

5. Slice the bagels in half and toast them. Once they're toasted, spread vegan butter on the bagel halves or drizzle with a teaspoon of extra virgin olive oil. Add the rocket to one of the bagel halves followed by the tempeh, and finish with the tomatoes on top.

6. Pop the lid on the bagel, pick it up, eat it, seize the day or go back to bed for an hour if you fancy it.

CALS: 844 | **PROTEIN:** 34g | **FAT:** 41g | **SAT FAT:** 6g | **CARBS:** 74g | **SUGAR:** 29g | **SALT:** 6.4g | **FIBRE:** 18g

POSH BEANS ON TOAST

Now everyone loves a particular brand of baked beans, which I will not name because I don't like lawsuits. But here's my way of saying to that particular tin, 'hey, you're great, but it's just not working out, I've found someone better who is a bit of me'. Who is that someone better? It's this recipe.

*5 mins prep + 14 mins cooking = **19 mins total***

SERVES 2–3

1 white onion
250g cherry tomatoes
2 tbsp light olive oil
2 garlic cloves
1 tsp smoked paprika
1 tsp dried mixed herbs
3 tbsp tomato paste
200ml hot water
1 x 400g tin butter beans
1 x 400g tin cannellini beans
2 tbsp balsamic vinegar
2 tbsp agave syrup
1–2 slices of sourdough bread
vegan butter or extra virgin
  olive oil, for the toast
salt and pepper

1. Dice the onion and halve those cherry tomatoes. Fry them both in a saucepan on a medium heat with olive oil for about 6–8 minutes until softened and the tomatoes are blistered and bubbling.

2. Next up, chop or grate the garlic cloves, then add them to the tomato and onion pan along with the paprika and dried herbs. Cook for another 2 minutes, then chuck in the tomato paste and the hot water. Leave it bubbling while you crack on with step 3.

3. Rinse and drain both tins of beans and add them to the saucepan. Give the beans a good season with salt and pepper, then add the vinegar and agave syrup. Let it bubble on a high heat for 4–6 minutes until the liquid has almost reduced and the beans are hot through and it looks like the baked beans we all know and love.

4. Finish the recipe by toasting the slices of bread, lathering them in vegan butter (or extra virgin olive oil), and topping it with the gorgeous beans.

5. You don't need to garnish this, or do anything apart from eat. So do that. And thank me later.

CALS: 768 | **PROTEIN:** 26g | **FAT:** 23g | **SAT FAT:** 4.4g | **CARBS:** 103g | **SUGAR:** 33g | **SALT:** 2.7g | **FIBRE:** 16g

MY SIMPLE TOFU SCRAMBLE

For when you fancy 'eggs'.

Here's an excellent recipe. And no doubt the response I'll get to this is, 'these aren't eggs', 'meh meh meh', 'it's just fried tofu', and they're correct. This brilliant tofu scramble brings me back to the time when I used to enjoy scrambled eggs. An honestly delicious alternative, it will take you no time at all. Best served with toast.

*4 mins prep + 12 mins cooking = **16 mins total***

SERVES 2

1 x 280g jar sun-dried tomatoes
3 spring onions
280g (1 block) extra-firm tofu
2 tsp ground turmeric
1 tsp ground cumin
1 tsp sweet smoked paprika
20ml oat milk
50g (handful) of baby spinach
2 slices of sourdough bread
vegan butter, for spreading
  (optional)
salt and pepper

1. Take 8 sun-dried tomatoes from the jar and slice them up with the spring onions. Get the tomatoes and the white parts of the spring onions frying on a medium–low heat in a large frying pan with 2 tablespoons of the oil from the jar of tomatoes. That oil is very tomatoey and flavoursome FYI.

2. Crumble the tofu into a bowl with your hands until you have little pieces that should resemble a scrambled egg. Add that to the frying pan and whack the heat up to medium. Season that up with a good pinch each of salt and pepper then add the spices in.

3. After about 5 minutes, once the tofu is golden and starting to crisp up, pour in the oat milk to stop things from sticking and also to help make the tofu slightly creamy.

4. Give it another season with salt and pepper, then chuck in the spinach and stir. I think this is a great time to toast the bread, don't you? Great. Toast your bread please.

5. Once toasted, spread with a good bit of vegan butter if you've got it. Top with your tofu scramble, one more season with salt and pepper and the green parts of the spring onion and you're good to go my friend.

CALS: 631 | **PROTEIN:** 22g | **FAT:** 37g | **SAT FAT:** 6.2g | **CARBS:** 48g | **SUGAR:** 3.7g | **SALT:** 2.1g | **FIBRE:** 9g

ONE-PAN BREAKFAST VEG MEDLEY

Sunshine in a pan.

A one-pan breakfast. It sounds too good to be true, I'm aware of that. But this works, everything in it works. It sort of reminds me of the shakshuka, but incorporates more of my favourite veggies, such as the courgette (or, if you're American, the zucchini). Anyways, give it a crack, and see how much you keep going back to this on your Saturday mornings.

*7 mins prep + 10 mins cooking = **17 mins total***

SERVES 2

3 portobello mushrooms (about 250g)
1 courgette
light olive oil, for frying
3 spring onions
2 jarred red peppers, drained
2 garlic cloves
2 tbsp tomato paste
1 x 400g tin cannellini beans
1 tsp smoked paprika
2 tsp dried mixed herbs
½ lemon
salt and pepper

To serve
2 slices sourdough bread
extra virgin olive oil, for drizzling

1. Chop up the mushrooms and the courgette into 1cm-thick slices (you can do it by eye, don't worry – I know you're not going to get a ruler out). Get that all in a nice large frying pan with a little light olive oil and fry on a medium heat, adding a pinch of salt to help draw the water out of the veggies – this is going to work wonders, trust me.

2. While that's frying, chop up the spring onions, including the greens, cut the peppers into slices and grate the garlic until it's as fine as me. Keep the green bits of the spring onion for later, then chuck the rest of it into the pan once the mushrooms and courgette are golden and crisp. Squeeze in the tomato paste at the same time and mix everything together.

3. Drain the cannellini beans using a sieve or colander, then add those to the pan. Mix them up so the veggies are having a nice chat with the cannellini beans, then give it a season and sprinkle in the paprika and mixed herbs. Stir it up well and cook for another few minutes until the beans are nice and almost fluffy inside.

4. You might want to toast your bread at this point.

5. Serve up the contents of the pan with your toast, adding a final pinch of salt and a little squeeze of lemon juice. Oh, and those green bits from the onion. Drizzle your bread with extra virgin olive oil and dip it into the veg medley, or spoon some of the veggies on top. Enjoy it.

CALS: 536 | **PROTEIN:** 20g | **FAT:** 16g | **SAT FAT:** 2.6g | **CARBS:** 72g | **SUGAR:** 17g | **SALT:** 4g | **FIBRE:** 10g

HEARTY SHAKSHUKA

Shake yourself into this shuka.

A one-pan delight, this hearty shakshuka is based on a classic Middle Eastern dish, and it's one that continues to come up in my weekend brunches. If you're not into dipping bread, then look away now.

*5 mins prep + 14 mins cooking = **19 mins total***

SERVES 2

1 white onion
2 jarred red peppers, drained
3 garlic cloves
a little olive oil, for frying
300g (1 block) silken tofu
2 tbsp tahini, plus extra for drizzling
juice of 1 lemon
2 tbsp tomato paste
1 tsp smoked paprika
1 x 400g tin chopped tomatoes
1 tbsp parsley
2 slices of sourdough bread or flatbreads
salt and pepper

1. Dice up the onion, red peppers and 2 of the garlic cloves, then whack a large frying pan on a medium heat with a little bit of olive oil. Chuck the onion, peppers and garlic into the pan and add a pinch of salt. Fry for 3–5 minutes until completely softened.

2. While that's cooking, in a food processor (yes, it's back) blitz the tofu, tahini, half the lemon juice and the remaining garlic clove together until smooth and season to taste with salt and pepper.

3. Dollop the tomato paste into the frying pan with the onion and peppers, add the paprika and fry for 1 more minute to let the paste and spice cook a little. Pour in the chopped tomatoes and add some water to the tin to fill it a quarter full. Pour the water into the pan, stir and let it bubble away for about 5 minutes until thickened.

4. Make little wells in the tomato mixture – it's easiest to do this using a silicone spatula – exposing the bottom of the frying pan if you can. One dip at a time, pour the silken tofu mix into the wells. Pop a lid on the pan, crank the heat down to a medium-low, and let the tops of the tofu cook for 3–4 minutes or until hardened.

5. While that's happening, chop up a bit of the parsley. As well as this, toast the bread. I mention this because you will forget to do this, let's face it.

6. Once everything's ready, sprinkle the parsley over the top, along with a little extra drizzle of tahini, the rest of the lemon juice and a crack of black pepper. Dip your toasted bread in and give it a go.

CALS: 650 | **PROTEIN:** 26g | **FAT:** 24g | **SAT FAT:** 3.4g | **CARBS:** 75g | **SUGAR:** 30g | **SALT:** 3.4g | **FIBRE:** 8.7g

QUICK EATS

2

THE MEALS YOU'D HAVE REGULARLY

They're quick, as you may have expected.

Well let's be fair, you'll probably have all the meals in this book all the time. These are the ones that I'd imagine you'd have for lunch, a quick dinner or double up as meal prep.

I'd say this is probably the section where you'll find yourself the most, purely because they're the recipes that I see you making often. Not to say you won't make the others in this book as often, but these ones you definitely will.

There's also, to your surprise, a few really good salad recipes. So try them while you're here.

CREAMY HARISSA CHICKPEA CIABATTAS

Harissa in a ciabatta? I call it ciabanter.

I do genuinely keep going back for this one. Roasting chickpeas is actually so simple to do, and honestly works wonders with a yogurty harissa sauce that's not too spicy yet has so much kick. I do believe you're gonna love this one like it's your second child, so enjoy.

*8 mins prep + 12 mins cooking = **20 mins total***

SERVES 2

baking paper (not an ingredient but something you may have to go to the shops and get)
extra virgin olive oil, for drizzling
1 x 400g tin chickpeas
2 tsp smoked paprika
1 tsp ground cumin
2 half ciabatta loaves
3 garlic cloves
2 tbsp rose harissa
1 tbsp tomato paste
200g vegan Greek-style yogurt
50ml hot water
1 lemon
8 small cherry vine tomatoes
handful of wild rocket
salt and pepper

1. Preheat your oven to 200°C (fan 180°C/gas mark 6). Line a baking tray with baking paper and use a little bit of oil in between the tray and the paper to help the paper stick. Then drain the chickpeas using a colander, shake dry and add to the tray.

2. Season the chickpeas with salt and pepper, drizzle with extra virgin olive oil and sprinkle with the spices. Mix together. Drizzle with some more extra virgin olive oil and pop in the oven for 12 minutes. It's that simple.

3. Slice the ciabattas in half on the longer side, so you have the top and the bottom in half, then drizzle with a touch of olive oil and pop them in the oven on a separate baking tray for 8 minutes.

4. Chop the garlic until finely diced, then fry in a large frying pan with a glug of olive oil on a medium heat. Once softened, dollop in the harissa and tomato paste and cook for 2 minutes. Muddle in the yogurt, add the hot water, mix away and let it bubble down until you have a thick yogurty sauce. Season to taste and add a squeeze of half a lemon to help balance everything out.

5. Once the chickpeas are roasted, carefully take them out of the oven as well as the ciabattas. Put the ciabatta on a plate and pop the chickpeas into the harissa yogurty sauce and mix well. And that's the recipe done.

6. Just kidding. Wow, what a joker I am. Slice your cherry tomatoes. Assemble your ciabattas with the rocket on the bottom, then the harissa chickpeas, then the sliced tomatoes and a squeeze of lemon juice. Top with the ciabatta. And that's the recipe actually done this time.

CALS: 512 | **PROTEIN:** 22g | **FAT:** 22g | **SAT FAT:** 3.1g | **CARBS:** 49g | **SUGAR:** 8.5g | **SALT:** 1.8g | **FIBRE:** 12g

ONE-POT BBQ MUSHROOM RICE BOWL

Tangy, warming, sensational.

This is essentially a preview if ever I was to do a one-pan, one-tray, one-utensil book. And I can promise you now, this is a beautiful way of having a scrummy rice bowl that's got banging flavour. The black beans and crispy mushrooms are a beautiful couple, they should get married, but when you smother it in the miso BBQ sauce, it is just perfect. Right from bottom to top.

*10 mins prep + 10 mins cooking = **20 mins total***

SERVES 2

200g exotic mixed mushrooms
a little light olive oil, for frying
1 x 400g tin black beans
1 tsp smoked paprika
2cm (¾in) piece of ginger
2 garlic cloves
1 tbsp red miso paste
3 tbsp dark soy sauce
2 tbsp apple cider vinegar
1 tbsp agave syrup
50ml water
1 x 250g pouch cooked basmati
   or wholegrain rice
salt and pepper

To serve
1 spring onion
1 lime
fresh coriander sprigs

1. Slice up the mushrooms into thin strips then grab yourself a large saucepan and fry the mushrooms on a medium heat with a little oil. It's also worth adding a pinch of salt as this helps draw out the water from the mushrooms. Once golden and crispy, or after 6 minutes for those following a stopwatch, drain the black beans and pop them into the same pan along with the smoked paprika. Turn the heat down to medium-low please.

2. While the mushrooms are cooking, grate the ginger and garlic until nice and fine, if that makes sense. Then, in a small jug, mix the miso paste, soy sauce, vinegar, agave syrup and that grated ginger and garlic. Add the water to the jug and mix well, then pour that into the pot and let it bubble away until the water has reduced.

3. Give the pot a season with salt and pepper then chuck in the pouch of rice and a splash of hot water to help steam up the rice. Stir it all up together and let the rice cook for a minute or two until it's fluffy and warmed all the way through. Now slice the spring onion, the lime and coriander. Top the pot with the chopped spring onion, coriander and a squeeze of lime juice.

4. Eat.

CALS: 493 | **PROTEIN:** 19g | **FAT:** 11g | **SAT FAT:** 1.8g | **CARBS:** 70g | **SUGAR:** 20g | **SALT:** 5.5g | **FIBRE:** 17g

DANNY DANNY NOODLES

I made up this recipe based on the beloved Dan Dan noodles, except I know they are nothing like Dan Dan noodles. So why the name? One of my best mates, known by the government as Daniel Roach, has been supporting me and been an absolute rock for me over the past decade now, and while I've got the opportunity, I thought I'd stick his name in a cookbook, because you only get one life and why not? Anyway, these noodles are absolutely sensational, and I can't wait for you to try them.

*6 mins prep + 12 mins cooking = **18 mins total***

SERVES 2

240g shiitake mushrooms
vegetable oil, for frying
4 spring onions
2cm (¾in) piece of ginger
2 garlic cloves
2 tsp Chinese five-spice
50g frozen edamame beans
3 tbsp dark soy sauce
1 tsp white or red miso paste
1 tbsp agave syrup
juice of ½ lime
300g ready-to-wok udon
  noodles

To serve
handful of fresh coriander
  (optional)
crunchy chilli oil (optional)
sesame seeds, to sprinkle

Named after my mate Danny, for no reason.

1. Chop up the mushrooms into small squares (known professionally as 'dice'). Shove that into a hot large frying pan over a medium heat with a little vegetable oil and fry for about 6 minutes until the mushrooms are golden and crispy.

2. Meanwhile, slice the spring onions, peel and grate the ginger and garlic, and put that into a little pile. Add the onions, ginger and garlic to the mushrooms and, at the same time, reduce the heat to a medium-low. After about 2 minutes, add the Chinese five-spice and the edamame beans into the mix and fry for about 3 minutes until everything's cooked.

3. In a small bowl, mix the soy sauce, miso paste, agave syrup and lime juice together until smooth.

4. Boil some water in a kettle, then remove the udon noodles from their packets and put them in a heatproof bowl. Pour the boiling water over the noodles and let it sit for 2 minutes.

5. Assembly time. Drain the noodles and pop them into the frying pan, along with the sauce and a splash of hot water. Mix until everything has come together and you're left with some sweet, sweet noodles.

6. Chop the coriander (if using) and top the noodles with it. Finish with some chilli oil if you like, the sesame seeds, and a final season with salt and pepper.

7. Get them in your gob.

CALS: 412 | **PROTEIN:** 19g | **FAT:** 8.8g | **SAT FAT:** 0.7g | **CARBS:** 59g | **SUGAR:** 18g | **SALT:** 4.6g | **FIBRE:** 12g

BOUJEE BLACK BEAN & QUINOA SALAD

Salad of a higher class.

I'll be honest, there is only one reason that this is called a boujee salad. For those who aren't down with the youths like myself, boujee is the word that basically means 'classy and excellent', and this salad is just that. It's the type of salad you'd see on a menu for £15.99 and you'd think 'ah, it's a bit expensive', but then you try it and go, 'wait, actually, this is proper'. So, do me a favour please, make it. Thank you in advance.

*5 mins prep + 15 mins cooking = **20 mins total***

SERVES 2

150g dry quinoa, washe
  in a sieve
1 vegan stock cube
1 red pepper
½ red onion
10g (handful of) fresh coriander
juice of 1 lime
1 x 400g tin black beans
2 tbsp smooth peanut butter
1 tbsp light soy sauce
1 tbsp sesame oil
1 tsp agave syrup
30ml warm water
a few roasted peanuts
  (about 5g), to serve
salt and pepper

1. Little saucepan out please. In that, add the washed quinoa and triple the amount of boiling water (so if you use 150g quinoa, add 450ml of water), and crumble in the stock cube. Let it boil on a high heat then turn the heat down to medium and cook for 12–15 minutes. Set a timer for this by the way, it'll help out a lot.

2. In that period of cooking, where you could once again do nothing, chop up the pepper and red onion into nice diced pieces, removing the core and seeds from the pepper. Also chop that coriander please. Pop those in a big salad bowl with half the lime juice and a pinch of salt and pepper.

3. Your quinoa is still cooking isn't it? Great. For the last 5 minutes of cooking, drain the black beans in a colander and add them to the quinoa to warm up a bit.

4. In a small jug, mix the peanut butter, soy sauce, sesame oil, the rest of the lime juice and the agave syrup until fully combined. Also chuck in the warm water to help make it dressing-like.

5. Quinoa done. Drain any excess water, if there is any, and mix the quinoa and black beans with the chopped veggies and herbs in the big salad bowl, and add three-quarters of the dressing. Toss like you'd usually toss a salad, then drizzle with the last bit of dressing. Crush a few peanuts over the top and maybe an extra flare of coriander on top.

6. And that, my friend, is it. Have it now, pop it in container with a lid for later, or serve it as part of a big feast for your mates and dates.

CALS: 640 | **PROTEIN:** 28g | **FAT:** 23g | **SAT FAT:** 4g | **CARBS:** 71g | **SUGAR:** 17g | **SALT:** 4.6g | **FIBRE:** 19g

SHREDDED CARROT SALAD

I have nothing else to say apart from my mum loves this, so you will too. It's nutty, it's fresh, and the crunchiness of the carrot with the zesty peanut dressing makes this an absolute winner.

8 mins prep + 5 mins cooking = 13 mins total

SERVES 2

3–4 medium carrots
80g frozen edamame beans
3 spring onions
½ cucumber
salt and pepper

For the dressing
2 tbsp smooth peanut butter
1 tbsp dark soy sauce
juice of 1 lime
1 tbsp apple cider vinegar
2 tbsp sesame oil
30ml hot water

To serve
pinch of fresh coriander
pinch of sesame seeds
pinch of crispy onions

1. Wash the carrots, then grate them using a box grater on the biggest-size holes you can. You essentially wanted good strands of carrots. Once you've got your carrots grated, pop them into a big bowl appropriate for salads.

2. Soak the edamame beans in a heatproof bowl of boiling water for 5 minutes.

3. Mix the peanut butter, soy sauce, lime juice, vinegar and sesame oil in a little dressing pot until fully combined. Add the hot water to help loosen it up into a lovely creamy consistency and so it's not splitting up like your favourite five-member boyband.

4. Cut the spring onions and cucumber into thin slices and drain the edamame, then mix them with the carrots. Now why not shove the rest of the ingredients in. Pour over three-quarters of the dressing and toss until everything is fully coated. Season quickly to taste, then serve the salad with everything I've listed to serve (obviously). Finish with the last quarter of dressing and you're done. Close this book and eat your salad.

A slaw for the history books.

CALS: 425 | **PROTEIN:** 12g | **FAT:** 30g | **SAT FAT:** 6g | **CARBS:** 21g | **SUGAR:** 17g | **SALT:** 1.8g | **FIBRE:** 11g

THE GO-TO GREENS SALAD

I'll be upfront: I'm not a salad man. If there was a side option, it would have to be fries, I don't care if that upsets the spinach lovers. But this is exactly the reason why: when I do make a salad, I want to make it a brilliant one, one I can enjoy and be floored by, and this is definitely one of those. And a sharp vinaigrette? Should be on all salads if you ask me.

It's all because of the dress(ing).

7 mins prep + 12 mins cooking = 19 mins total

SERVES 2

2 baby shallots or 1 banana shallot (if you can't find either, ½ red onion works)
2 lemons, plus more if you want to finish the salad with it
150g tenderstem broccoli
baking paper (not an ingredient but something you may have to go to the shops and get)
4 tbsp extra virgin olive oil, plus extra for roasting
50g frozen edamame beans
5 tbsp tahini
2 tbsp apple cider vinegar
1 x 400g tin chickpeas
150g spinach, washed please (do you live at a festival?)
a small handful of fresh basil (optional)
salt and pepper

TOP TIP:

If you can't eat tahini, no problem! At step one, add the olive oil and mix well, then blitz for a smooth vinaigrette or leave it chunky.

1. Oven. On. 200°C (fan 180°C/gas mark 6). First things first; chop the shallots into tiny diced pieces and pop into a jar or little jug. Squeeze the juice from both lemons over the shallots and pop a good pinch of salt in too. Let it sit for a bit.

2. Next, cut the tenderstem broccoli stalks in half, shove them on a baking tray lined with baking paper or foil, then season with salt and pepper, drizzle with olive oil and roast for 12 minutes.

3. Okay, now put the edamame in a heatproof bowl and cover with boiling water. That should cook the edamame all the way through and take about 5 minutes.

4. You've done a lot haven't you? Sorry, but it's so worth it. In a food processor, blitz the shallots and the liquid in the jar or little jug with the olive oil and tahini. Season it to taste, then add the apple cider vinegar, blitz once more and boom – dressing done. You should have a dressing that's not too thick and has a nice sharpness thanks to the lemon juice (chef words).

5. Drain the edamame and the chickpeas together in a colander then throw them in a big salad bowl with the spinach and cooked broccoli. Toss together then tear in the basil leaves (if using).

6. Finally, lovingly pour over the creamy shallot dressing and toss once more (cheeky).

7. Squeeze a bit more lemon juice over the salad if you fancy a bit more of a fresh zing, but your job is complete, you've just made a banger of a salad.

CALS: 746 | **PROTEIN:** 26g | **FAT:** 57g | **SAT FAT:** 7.9g | **CARBS:** 22g | **SUGAR:** 4g | **SALT:** 0.35g | **FIBRE:** 15g

SHREDDED TOFU FAJITAS

I know that you might not, until today, have used your cheese grater for anything else apart from cheese. However, this recipe is in the dictionary under the word 'gamechanger'. Don't believe me? Fajita it up. On another note, it's funny to say the word 'fajita' in an Irish accent but pronouncing the J.

You'll need a cheese grater.

8 mins prep + 12 mins cooking = 20 mins total

SERVES 2

1 red onion
1 red pepper
125g shiitake mushrooms
light olive oil, for frying
280g (1 block) extra-firm tofu
2 garlic cloves
3 tbsp dark soy sauce
2 tsp dried mixed herbs
2 tsp smoked paprika
2 tsp ground cumin
2 tbsp tomato paste
2 wholemeal tortilla wraps
salt and pepper

To serve
2 tbsp vegan Greek-style yogurt
drizzle of chilli sauce (I like Tabasco)
pinch of fresh coriander
a few romaine lettuce leaves

1. Slice up the onion, pepper and mushrooms into thin strips (discarding the core and seeds from the pepper), then fry them both in the large frying pan you should already have out by now for around 6–8 minutes. As per usual, medium heat with a little bit of oil. It's also worth adding a pinch of salt as that helps draw out the water from the mushrooms.

2. Grab a box grater and grate the extra-firm tofu like it's a block of cheese until you get through the entire block. Grate the garlic cloves with the same grater on the smaller holes while you're at it.

3. When the veggies have softened, season them then chuck in the grated tofu, garlic, soy sauce, dried herbs and the spices. Stir and cook for 2–3 minutes.

4. When your tofu strips are warmed through, pop in the tomato paste and season with salt and pepper. If the tofu and veggies are sticking at this point, add a splash of water to help stop that from happening.

5. Toast up your tortillas in a frying pan on high heat for less than 30 seconds each side. Alternatively, you can do this in half the time by cooking the tortillas directly over the gas flame, turning them with tongs, if you have a gas hob.

6. Now serve, with whatever you want on top, including but not limited to the listed toppings, and make it look lovely your own way. Or, if you can't be bothered to get creative, copy the photo.

TOP TIP:

This will also work really well if you wanted to use romaine lettuce leaves as wraps.

CALS: 501 | **PROTEIN:** 27g | **FAT:** 18g | **SAT FAT:** 3.3g | **CARBS:** 51g | **SUGAR:** 20g | **SALT:** 5.3g | **FIBRE:** 14g

'CHUNA' SANDWICH

Let's face it, tuna is great in a sandwich. Unless you don't like fish. Well, if you don't, hello babe, join the club. This one changes the game, flips it over, and makes it vegan. Don't go in expecting a like-for-like tuna, because this is its own thing entirely. And, as expected by vegans, it is made with chickpeas for the protein, and jackfruit for the texture. And that's why, in typical pronunciation from anywhere south in England, I've called it 'chuna'. Enjoy in a sandwich, wrap or as a salad topping.

*10 mins prep + 3 mins making = **13 mins total***

SERVES 2

4 tbsp tahini
juice of 1 lemon
70ml hot water
1 x 400g tin chickpeas
1 x 400g tin jackfruit
2 tbsp caper brine (the liquid from a jar of capers)
½ cucumber
1 beef tomato
1 head little gem lettuce
4 slices farmhouse bread (white crusty bread)
salt and pepper

No fishy business about it.

1. In a small bowl, mix the tahini with the lemon juice, a pinch of salt and the hot water until you end up with a runny tahini sauce. (If you prefer you could use vegan mayo instead of this tahini sauce and skip this step.)

2. Drain the chickpeas and jackfruit in a colander, making sure to take any of the hard stems or seeds off the jackfruit and discard them.

3. Add the drained chickpeas, jackfruit, caper brine and three-quarters of the tahini sauce (or all the mayo) to a food processor and give it five or so pulses. You want the texture to be just like tuna; smooth but still chunky. Season to taste with salt and pepper.

4. Cut the cucumber and tomato into thin slices and chop up the lettuce into thin strips while you've got the knife in your hand as well. Thank you.

5. Lightly toast your bread in the toaster if you fancy it. Now assemble. Spread the remaining quarter of tahini sauce (or, again, the mayo) on two of the slices of bread, then add the lettuce, tomatoes, 'chuna', and finally the cucumber.

6. Add the remaining two slices of bread on top and you've got a sarnie that's absolutely lovely.

CALS: 716 | **PROTEIN:** 28g | **FAT:** 27g | **SAT FAT:** 3.8g | **CARBS:** 78g | **SUGAR:** 9.4g | **SALT:** 2.2g | **FIBRE:** 20g

ACTUALLY, A DECENT TOMATO SALAD

A change from the head to-may-toes.

Welcome to a tomato salad, typical you might say, for a boy who eats grass? But nein. This is a fresh, zingy and almighty tomato salad, that goes beyond the average one you might get offered as the vegan option at a BBQ. The bold dressing complements the tomatoes brilliantly, and the addition of crunchy chickpeas adds a new texture that'll get you loving salad again. Bring this along to any event, and it's also best made when it's summer. Or when you fancy a freshen up.

*7 mins prep + 12 mins cooking = **19 mins total***

SERVES 2

baking paper (not an ingredient but something you may have to go to the shops and get)
4 tbsp extra virgin olive oil for the salad, plus extra for drizzling
1 x 400g tin chickpeas
2 tsp smoked paprika
1 tsp ground cumin
1 tsp dried mixed herbs
2 large tomatoes
½ red onion
2 tbsp balsamic vinegar
½ cucumber
handful of fresh mint
½ lime
salt and pepper

1. Whack the oven on at 200°C (fan 180°C/gas mark 6) please. Line a tray with baking paper, using a little bit of oil in between the tray and the paper to help the paper stick. Then drain the chickpeas using a colander, shake dry and add to the tray.

2. Season the chickpeas with salt and pepper, drizzle with extra virgin olive oil, add the spices and mixed herbs, and mix together. Pop in the oven for 12 minutes.

3. Now the tomatoes. Cut them up into nice small chunks, give them a quick season and chuck them into a salad bowl, then do the exact same chopping technique for the red onion without crying. Unless you've got *Stranger Things* season 4 episode 9 on in the background. Lather them both in the balsamic vinegar and a good pinch of salt, mix together and let it sit. When mixing, make sure the onions separate, like a flower shedding its petals.

4. Now cut the cucumber in half, then into small pieces, and why not do the mint as well and chop that up finely. Chuck the cucumber (not the mint) into the bowl and toss gently together.

5. At this point, the chickpeas should be ready. Let them cool a bit then add them into the bowl with the tomatoes. Finish with the olive oil, a good squeeze of lime juice, a good pinch of salt and pepper and that's it.

6. OMG NO it's NOT! I FORGOT THE MINT, yeah add the mint on top, bosh.

CALS: 545 | **PROTEIN:** 12g | **FAT:** 37g | **SAT FAT:** 5g | **CARBS:** 33g | **SUGAR:** 15g | **SALT:** 0.3g | **FIBRE:** 11g

MISO ME UP STIR-FRY

A bit of mi in your life.

By now, you might have already clocked that I use a lot of miso in my recipes. And one of my core principles in this book is using ingredients that you're going to be eating on a regular basis. Miso paste is made of fermented beans, usually soy beans, and brings such a brilliant depth of flavour. And that's why you need a bit of this in your life. Such as this simple stir-fry.

*8 mins prep + 10 mins cooking = **18 mins total***

SERVES 2

200g tenderstem broccoli
3 spring onions, white parts only
120g shiitake mushrooms
vegetable or sesame oil, for frying
3cm (1¼in) piece of ginger
1 tbsp red miso paste
3 tbsp apple cider vinegar
1 tbsp agave syrup
50ml hot water
65g (handful of) spring greens (or kale), shredded
100g frozen edamame beans
handful of beansprouts
2 packs of ready-to-wok medium thread noodles (if you fancy them)
salt and pepper

To serve
sesame seeds
fresh coriander

1. Chop up the broccoli, spring onions and mushrooms into small bite-size pieces, then chuck them all into a large frying pan on a medium heat with a bit of veggie or sesame oil. Add a quick pinch each of salt and pepper and fry it up for 5 minutes or until golden.

2. Next, grate the ginger and then mix the miso paste, vinegar and agave syrup in a small jug with the hot water. Leave it to the side but tell it not to worry as you're coming back for it later.

3. Add the spring greens, edamame beans and beansprouts to the frying pan and mix well, making sure everything cooks up nicely, then pour the miso sauce in lovingly, and stir it up. Give it another season for good luck.

4. If you're not having noodles, skip this babe. Finish the recipe by popping in the ready-to-wok noodles and a splash of hot water, then stirring everything up together.

5. Top with sesame seeds and tear some coriander leaves over the top. Stop reading this now, go eat.

CALS: 515 | **PROTEIN:** 27g | **FAT:** 14g | **SAT FAT:** 1.4g | **CARBS:** 62g | **SUGAR:** 16g | **SALT:** 1.7g | **FIBRE:** 15g

READY RED PEPPER PASTA

Let's get ready to pepper.

The joke makes no sense, but the dish does. This is easily one of my favourite renditions of making pasta. That's it, that's all I have to say.

*6 mins prep + 14 mins cooking = **20 mins total***

SERVES 2

200g linguine (or any other pasta you want)
4 jarred red peppers, drained
1 white onion
2 garlic cloves
light olive oil, for frying
pinch of chilli flakes
1 tsp dried mixed herbs
10g fresh basil, plus extra to serve
150g (about ½ block) silken tofu
4 tbsp nutritional yeast
salt and pepper

1. The first step to any pasta recipe of mine is exactly the same. Boil water, salt water, put pasta in water, cook until pasta is al dente. Happy days.

2. Next up, dice up the jarred red peppers with the onion and garlic. Add it all to a large frying pan with a little bit of oil on a medium heat and fry until it's all golden and the onion and garlic have softened.

3. After a minute of those peppers and garlic getting to know each other, add the chilli flakes and dried herbs and tear in the fresh basil leaves. Whack that heat down to low and stir well. Also, at this point, add a good pinch each of salt and pepper please. Trust me.

4. Once everything has softened, add the entire contents of the pan to a food processor, along with the silken tofu and the nutritional yeast. Give it a blitz and, once smooth, pour lovingly back into the pan. You might not need all of it so don't get overconfident thinking you've smashed it.

5. Now your pasta's cooked, grab a mug of pasta water (around 100ml) then drain the pasta in a colander. Add the pasta to the peppery sauce and then about half the reserved pasta water. Mix well until the pasta is coated in the silky and gorgeous sauce. Then serve in bowls with a sprig of basil and a quick season please. And you're done.

CALS: 669 | **PROTEIN:** 31g | **FAT:** 13g | **SAT FAT:** 1.6g | **CARBS:** 101g | **SUGAR:** 29g | **SALT:** 4.2g | **FIBRE:** 12g

SIMPLY, A NOODLE SOUP

This soup should only be consumed when it's cold outside. So, if you're reading this in England, make this between October and May, and if you're in Scotland, you can make this all year round. If ever you're after a cracking noodle soup, and you're happy when there's no strictness as to what's in that soup, then this recipe is for you. I do make this one a lot, so I hope you enjoy it as much as I do. Also, the veggies I've used are completely interchangeable, so if you've got some spare carrots, or spare peppers, throw them in too.

*7 mins prep + 12 mins cooking = **19 mins total***

SERVES 2

4 spring onions
1 medium carrot
2 garlic cloves
150g tenderstem broccoli
light olive oil, for frying
2½ tsp white miso paste
1.2 litres hot veggie stock
 (boiling water plus 3 stock cubes)
100g cavolo nero or posh kale
100g dried wholewheat soba noodles
80g frozen peas
80g frozen sweetcorn
2cm (¾in) piece of ginger
2 tbsp mirin
1 tbsp dark soy sauce (optional)
salt and pepper
fresh coriander, to serve

1. Chop up the spring onions, carrot and garlic into thin slices, and the broccoli simply into little chunks.

2. Get a large saucepan on a medium heat and pour in a drizzle of light olive oil, then chuck in the spring onions, carrot and garlic. Give it a good season and cook for 3–5 minutes until just about golden.

3. Next, in a large jug, stir the miso paste into the hot stock and pour that into the large saucepan. Stir everything up and let it bubble for a good 5 minutes.

4. While that's happening, chop up the cavolo nero or kale leaves into nice thin slices. Then add those leaves, the noodles and the peas and sweetcorn into the saucepan. Finally, grate the ginger and add it to the soup at the end before everything is cooked, as well as the mirin (and the dark soy sauce if you need it saltier).

5. Let everything cook up and once the noodles are cooked, you're ready to serve.

6. Pour the noodles and broth carefully into bowls, using tongs for noodles and a ladle for the broth I reckon, and top with fresh coriander, some black pepper, and a smile.

7. Eat with a spoon, or a fork, or probably both.

Essentially, all your spare veg, but uplifted.

CALS: 495 | **PROTEIN:** 20g | **FAT:** 12g | **SAT FAT:** 1.4g | **CARBS:** 67g | **SUGAR:** 17g | **SALT:** 9.5g | **FIBRE:** 14g

SPICED-UP FRIED RICE

This is essentially your classic fried rice, made completely plant-based, with some bold pick-ups from myself. You can use any veg you fancy, but make sure you chop these as small as you possibly can.

*5 mins prep + 11 mins cooking = **16 mins total***

SERVES 2

4 spring onions
1 red pepper
2 garlic cloves
2cm (¾in) piece of ginger
light olive oil, for frying
2 tsp Chinese five-spice
4 tbsp light soy sauce
4 tbsp tahini
2 tbsp hot water
1 x 250g pouch cooked
  wholegrain rice
80g frozen edamame beans
50g frozen peas
15g fresh coriander
1 lime
Spinach Satay Side, to serve
  (see page 194, optional)

1. Slice up the spring onions. Deseed the red pepper and chop the garlic, ginger and red pepper into tiny pieces. Fry the spring onions and red pepper in a large frying pan with a drizzle of oil for a few minutes on a medium-high heat. Once golden, chuck in the garlic, ginger and Chinese five-spice.

2. In a lovely little bowl, mix the soy sauce, tahini and hot water to form a drizzle or sauce.

3. Add the cooked rice to the frying pan along with the frozen edamame beans and peas, a splash of hot water and the tahini–soy drizzle. Mix until combined. You'll know when you're done when the peas and edamame are cooked and the rice is fluffy. Once that happens, chop up the coriander and stir half of it into the rice.

4. Serve in a dressy bowl or plate with a squeeze of lime and the rest of the chopped coriander. This is lovely on its own but also great served with my Spinach Satay Side.

5. Take a step to admire what you made, then devour.

Did somebody order a Chinese?

CALS: 574 | **PROTEIN:** 20g | **FAT:** 33g | **SAT FAT:** 4.7g | **CARBS:** 44g | **SUGAR:** 13g | **SALT:** 5g | **FIBRE:** 11g

CREAMY SPINACH QUESADILLAS

A sensational toasted wrap.

Quesadillas are essentially beautiful toasted wraps, usually made with cheese, which we cannot have in this book because you picked up a vegan cookbook and I am, surprise surprise, a vegan. Which is why this recipe uses the humble silken tofu to substitute the ooziness that cheese would give you.

*5 mins prep + 10 mins cooking = **15 mins total***

SERVES 2

150g (about ½ block) silken tofu
30g (handful of) unsalted
   cashews
4 tbsp nutritional yeast
1 tsp Dijon mustard (optional,
   but gives a nice tangy flavour)
1 tsp red miso paste
light olive oil, for frying
2 garlic cloves
3 big handfuls (150g) baby
   spinach
1 lime
a few splashes of Tabasco
   (optional)
2 tortilla wraps (wholemeal
   ideally, but you can use the
   standard white if you like)
salt and pepper
handful of fresh coriander,
   to serve

1. Blitz up all the tofu ingredients like all the other recipes have shown you. In case you've chosen this as your first recipe (hello, hi, my name's Calum), get a food processor and add the silken tofu, cashews, nutritional yeast, mustard (if using) and miso paste and blitz until smooth. Set aside while you get on with the fun bit.

2. Chuck a drizzle of olive oil in a large frying pan and heat on a medium heat. Next, grate your garlic until it's nice and fine then fry it in the olive oil with the baby spinach. Cook until the spinach has essentially turned into nothing. Well, not nothing, just fully reduced. Cut the lime in half and add a squeeze of juice, add the Tabasco (if using) and a good pinch each of salt and pepper. Remove from the pan and pop into a bowl please.

3. Chuck a tortilla in that now empty pan on a medium heat and get ready to top it. Add half the spinach mix to one half of the tortilla and pour blobs of silken tofu on top of that. Do not, I repeat do not, overfill the quesadillas. I have made that mistake before.

4. After a minute of the wrap being on the heat, fold the plain uncovered side of the tortilla on top of the spinachy mixture. Press down gently, then after a few seconds, flip and leave on the heat for a minute more. You are aiming for golden, beautifully toasted sides. Repeat with the second tortilla and the rest of the filling.

5. Finish off the quesadillas by splitting them in half with a knife. Top with some fresh coriander and a squeeze of juice from the other half of the lime. You can also throw splashes of Tabasco on top as if you own the place. But yeah, done, go eat.

Quick Eats

CALS: 482 | **PROTEIN:** 27g | **FAT:** 23g | **SAT FAT:** 4.2g | **CARBS:** 36g | **SUGAR:** 6.9g | **SALT:** 1.7g | **FIBRE:** 9.7g

QUICKER NUTTY RAMEN

Now this is not a traditional ramen, nor is it an authentic ramen. It is essentially a beautiful, nutty noodle soup that anyone would fight to have you make for them. So, do me a massive favour, wait till the weather is below 10°C and get in the kitchen and make this.

*8 mins prep + 17 mins cooking = **25 mins total** (Slightly longer recipe)*

SERVES 2

2 garlic cloves
2cm (¾in) piece of ginger
4 spring onions
1 red chilli
2 tbsp sesame oil
125g shiitake mushrooms
4 tbsp dark soy sauce
2 tbsp agave syrup
2 veggie stock cubes
100g mangetout
80g edamame beans
300g ready-to-wok medium
   noodles
2 tbsp smooth peanut butter
2 tbsp red miso paste

To serve
fresh coriander
a pinch of sesame seeds
chilli oil (optional)

Noodles in a pot never looks so good.

1. Grate the garlic and ginger with a box grater, and pop half into a small bowl. Then chop up the white parts of the spring onions and chilli (deseed it if you can't handle the heat). Fry the chilli, spring onions and the other half of the ginger and garlic in a large frying pan on a medium heat with the sesame oil for 2–3 minutes until golden.

2. Chop up your mushrooms into nice thin slices and just leave them alone. They've been through a lot. Once the chilli, onions, garlic and ginger are golden, chuck the mushrooms in and fry for 6–8 minutes until crisp. Then add the soy sauce and 1 tablespoon of the agave syrup and reduce the heat.

3. Boil about 750ml of water in a kettle and add that to a large saucepan, then crumble in the stock cubes. Put the mangetout, edamame and noodles in a metal colander, then put the colander on top of the saucepan, so it covers the stock, adding the pan lid on top of that. Steam for 8 minutes. You're essentially steaming up and cooking everything without getting the veg lost in the stock.

4. Mix the peanut butter and miso paste with the rest of the garlic and ginger in the small bowl, along with the remaining tablespoon of agave syrup. That's your base.

5. Now for serving up. In the bowl you're going to serve the ramen in, add 2 tablespoons of peanut butter paste, then pour a bit of the stock water (around 50ml) in that bowl and mix together. Then fill the bowl with your desired amount of stock and get ready for the final bit. Repeat with a second bowl.

6. Lower in your noodles first using tongs or two forks, then top with the mangetout, edamame, your mushrooms, fresh coriander and the green parts of the spring onions and sesame seeds. You can add more toppings if you'd like, maybe some chilli oil, but the ramen is great as it was. As it was. As it was. You know it's not the same … Sorry. Eat the ramen, report back what you think.

CALS: 757 | **PROTEIN:** 30g | **FAT:** 34g | **SAT FAT:** 5.6g | **CARBS:** 77g | **SUGAR:** 29g | **SALT:** 11.9g | **FIBRE:** 12g

SUNNY TOMATO PESTO LINGUINE

For when the weather hits 18°C.

I think you might've gathered that I like pasta. And I do believe pesto is the elite pasta sauce. Why? Well, one – it's fresh, two – it's got so much flavour and, three – if you don't use it all, you can pop it in the fridge and it'll sit for a week and mind its business while you cheat on it with other dishes. This pesto is bursting full of sun-dried tomatoes, and gives you that feeling like it's 26°C even when it is winter when you're making it. It's also one of those filling pastas that you'll crave after a day of running about, doing everything under the sun.

*6 mins prep + 12 mins cooking = **18 mins total***

SERVES 3

200g linguine
140g sun-dried tomatoes
40g (handful of) unsalted
  cashews
25g fresh basil
10g fresh mint
5 tbsp nutritional yeast
1 garlic clove
4 tbsp extra virgin olive oil
25ml (a shot glass) ice-cold
  water
1 lemon
salt and pepper

To serve
fresh basil leaves
The Parmigiano Alternativo
  (page 212)

1. The obvious step in every single pasta recipe that I have to keep writing, even though you know exactly what it's going to be ... right. Start by heating your oven – I'M JOKING. Cook your pasta in salted boiling water in a large saucepan. Until it's ready. Every dried pasta is different, but 12 minutes is the standard time for perfect pasta.

2. Next up, your food processor or blender. Pop in all the remaining ingredients (except the lemon juice) and blitz until smooth. Season to taste with salt, pepper and the juice of the lemon.

3. When your pasta is nearly cooked, fill a mug with some pasta cooking water, then drain the pasta when it's cooked.

4. Throw it back – wait, no – throw the pasta in the saucepan along with the pesto and some of the reserved pasta cooking water. Stir on a low heat until the pesto has turned into a lovely and silky sauce.

5. Serve your pasta in nice bowls, topping it with some fresh basil and The Parmigiano Alternativo, which you'll find towards the back of this book. Bye.

CALS: 844 | **PROTEIN:** 26g | **FAT:** 54g | **SAT FAT:** 7.5g | **CARBS:** 55g | **SUGAR:** 7.3g | **SALT:** 1.5g | **FIBRE:** 16g

GREEN GODDESS SOUP

Green and not that mean, actually

One of the great things about cooking with more veg is finding ways of sneaking it into dishes, making you enjoy them more than you ever thought you would. Hence this soup. It wasn't invented by a Green Goddess, unless you count me as one, but it sure belongs on the plate of one. It's creamy, it's green, it's got so much goodness that I want to say more about it, but I have a word limit, so go make it. Again, it's good soup.

*4 mins prep + 15 mins cooking = **19 mins total***

SERVES 2

600g Maris Piper potatoes
6 spring onions (white parts only)
4 garlic cloves
light olive oil, for frying
1.5 litres veggie stock (3 stock cubes dissolved in 1.5 litres of boiling water)
15g fresh mint
400g frozen peas
200g baby spinach
15g fresh basil
15g fresh parsley
salt and pepper

To serve
½ lemon (optional)
drizzle of chilli oil (optional)
2 slices of sourdough bread

1. Peel the potatoes and chop them up into small cubes. Chop up the spring onions and garlic into rough slices. Fry them all with a pinch of salt and pepper in a large saucepan with a drizzle of olive oil on a medium-high heat for a few minutes until the onions have softened.

2. This is a great time to pour in 1.2 litres of the stock, keep back the other 300ml. Give it 10 minutes for the potatoes to cook all the way through. While you're waiting, strip the mint leaves from the stalks.

3. Now the potatoes should be cooked. At this point, add your frozen peas and the entirety-of-your-life-savings-worth of spinach.

4. Once the peas are cooked and the spinach is wilted, add the mint leaves, basil and parsley to the pan then blitz the entire contents of the saucepan in a large food processor, or use a hand-held blender if you've got one. Add a generous season of salt and pepper, trust me. Blitz until the soup is smooth and use the extra stock to loosen it if too thick.

5. Pour the luscious green soup into nice warm bowls and top if off with a final season of salt and pepper and a squeeze of lemon juice, or if you're feeling up to it, chilli oil. Serve with some good-old bread. Well, not old bread, I mean fresh bread, that's good and old like your nan.

TOP TIP:

The Parmigiano Alternativo (see page 212) also works as a topping for this one.

CALS: 718 | **PROTEIN:** 31g | **FAT:** 11g | **SAT FAT:** 1.7g | **CARBS:** 115g | **SUGAR:** 16g | **SALT:** 3.4g | **FIBRE:** 18g

THAI-STYLE PEANUT BUTTER CURRY

Spicy, creamy, and a bit of you.

There is someone out there who can smash this recipe and make it truly authentic. But for me, plant-based cooking is designed to change tradition, and this curry is one example where you'll try it and go 'That vegan bloke's right'. It's comforting, filling and has just enough spice, to make it very nice.

*6 mins prep + 14 mins cooking = **20 mins total***

SERVES 2

4 spring onions (white parts only)
1 courgette
3 garlic cloves
2cm (¾in) piece of ginger
light olive oil, for frying
3 tbsp Thai red curry paste
    (always check the label to
    make sure it's vegan)
1 x 160g tin of coconut cream
200ml veggie stock (or ½ stock
    cube dissolved in 200ml
    boiling water)
2 tbsp crunchy peanut butter
    (or almond or cashew butter)
1 x 400g tin chickpeas
1 red pepper
1 lime
1 tbsp light soy sauce
1 tbsp agave syrup
100g (big handful of) baby
    spinach
30g (handful of) unsalted
    cashews
1 x 250g pouch cooked jasmine
    rice
salt and pepper
fresh coriander, to serve

1. Chop up the spring onions and courgette into thin slices, then grate the garlic and ginger. In a large frying pan, add everything you just chopped with a drizzle of oil on a medium heat. Fry for 4–6 minutes until everything's softened and golden-ish.

2. Once everything's softened, chuck in the Thai red curry paste, the coconut cream and the veggie stock and stir until everything is well mixed. Next, stir in the nut butter.

3. Now back to prepping, mate. Drain the tin of chickpeas in a colander, then deseed the red pepper and chop it into nice chunks. While you're holding the knife, split the lime in half. Chuck the chickpeas and pepper chunks into the pan. Give the curry a season.

4. Let everything bubble away until the curry starts to thicken up and you have nicely cooked peppers that still have a little bit of crunch. If the curry is too thick, add water by all means.

5. Now for the last bits. Add the soy sauce and agave syrup to the curry as well as all that spinach, and a squeeze of half the lime. Crank the heat down to low and let it simmer until the spinach has completely cooked.

6. Toast the cashews in a small saucepan until they've got a good colour on them.

7. Now to serve. Pop the rice into the microwave for 90 seconds at 900W or whatever your packet and machine says to do. Top the curry with fresh coriander, the toasted cashews, which you can crumble on top, and a squeeze of the other half of that lime. Serve directly from the pan with the rice in a bowl on the side. Boom.

CALS: 940 | **PROTEIN:** 26g | **FAT:** 52g | **SAT FAT:** 21g | **CARBS:** 85g | **SUGAR:** 18g | **SALT:** 4.1g | **FIBRE:** 12g

GARLICKY TERIYAKI STIR-FRY

This is one for the scrapbook.

I love a great stir-fry. Nine times out of ten, unless I'm making something for mates or family, I don't end up making an extravagant meal for myself. And I guess a lot of people might be the same. So, for those wondering, if there is a meal that I keep coming back to, on a regular basis, or when I want a great simple meal, I go for this.

6 mins prep + 12 mins cooking = 18 mins total

SERVES 2

280g (1 block) extra-firm tofu
30g cornflour
a little light olive oil, for frying
3 spring onions
1 carrot
1 red pepper
300g ready-to-wok medium noodles
salt and pepper
sesame seeds, to serve

For the teriyaki sauce
3 garlic cloves
4 tbsp dark soy sauce
1 tbsp mirin
1½ tbsp agave syrup
50ml water

1. Crumble the tofu into a bowl in little bits. Next up, grab a bowl with a lid (or a big Tupperware – personally I like to use a takeaway container) and pop the cornflour in with a pinch each of salt and pepper. Chuck in the tofu, close the lid and shake to coat all of the pieces.

2. Fry the cornflour-coated tofu in a large frying pan on a medium heat with a little oil for about 6 minutes until all the pieces are crispy and crunchy. Now chop the spring onions and carrot into thin slices, and deseed the pepper and chop it into little chunks. Keep the green bits of the spring onion. Chuck those into the frying pan with the noodles, give everything a quick season and cook up the veg for about 3–4 minutes until softened but with a bit of bite.

3. Now for the teriyaki sauce. Let's peel the garlic and grate it using a box grater, then mix that and the soy, mirin, agave syrup and water in a small jug until combined.

4. Pour the teriyaki sauce over the veggies and stir well until the sauce has thickened and coated everything. I think that's it.

5. Serve yourself up a plate or a bowl of veggies, tofu and noodles and top with sesame seeds and the green parts of the spring onion. That's all for this.

CALS: 504 | **PROTEIN:** 17g | **FAT:** 14g | **SAT FAT:** 2.4g | **CARBS:** 73g | **SUGAR:** 26g | **SALT:** 5.5g | **FIBRE:** 8.4g

I don't usually wear rings
when chopping but may as
well chop in style, am I right?

TOFU SHISH KEBABS

I love a good kebab, and shish kebabs are pretty satisfying to make. You don't need a lot of prep for these, and genuinely speaking, the result is wonderful. Enjoy it and come back to me with a message that says 'Oh wow, the shish kebabs tho' when you do.

10 mins prep + 10 mins cooking = 20 mins total

SERVES 2

280g (1 block) smoked or regular extra-firm tofu
1 red pepper
1 yellow pepper
125g shiitake mushrooms
2 metal skewers (yes this is an ingredient)
olive oil, for drizzling
salt and pepper

For the marinade
1 lemon
100g vegan Greek-style yogurt, plus 1 tbsp for drizzling
1 tbsp extra virgin olive oil
2 tbsp rose harissa
1 garlic clove

To serve
100g rocket
1 tbsp olive oil
lemon wedges (optional)
2 pittas
Tahini Sauce (see page 214)

1. First, the tofu. Quickly drain and then chop up the tofu into 5mm-thick slices, please. Deseed the peppers and chop into cubes and remove the stalks from the mushrooms and leave them whole.

2. Next up, marination. Cut the lemon in half. In a large shallow bowl, add the yogurt, olive oil, harissa, juice of ½ lemon, and grate in the garlic clove too. Mix. Season with loads of salt and pepper then add the tofu to the bowl and coat the tofu slices in the marinade with your hands. It's okay if there is breakage of the slices.

3. Your oven should have a grill setting (it should look like a zig-zag line). Whack it onto the highest setting then get a baking sheet and line it with foil. Cheers for that.

4. Skewer the bits of veg and marinated tofu slices onto the metal skewers, folding the slices in half if they're too big. Go in any order you like. Once complete, lay them on the baking sheet. Season with salt and pepper, drizzle with a touch of olive oil, and grill for 8 minutes, turning halfway through.

5. While they're cooking, get the rocket into a bowl and add the juice of the remaining ½ lemon, as well as the tablespoon of olive oil, and a pinch of salt. Toss until everything's all coated. You might also want to toast your pittas – you can do this in a toaster or even a frying pan.

6. When the skewers are looking charred and crispy, take the sheet out from the grill, with oven gloves obviously (don't burn your hands), and leave to one side.

7. Open up your pittas, stuff them with rocket, and some Tahini Sauce too, then, when the skewers are cool, remove the veg and tofu from them and stuff them into the pitta. Drizzle on some extra yogurt and you're good to go … and eat.

CALS: 694 | **PROTEIN:** 30g | **FAT:** 37g | **SAT FAT:** 5.5g | **CARBS:** 53g | **SUGAR:** 14g | **SALT:** 2.3g | **FIBRE:** 15g

FIERY CHILLI PASTA

Spicier than Posh Spice.

Some people will already know this recipe. It's a creamy chilli pasta, with a crunchy garlicky breadcrumb topping to finish. It is sort of like a carbonara, if it fused with the Spice Girls. And like the Spice Girls, it is properly indulgent, and you'll wanna be its lover. Not in a weird way.

*4 mins prep + 12 mins cooking = **16 mins total***

SERVES 2

250g linguine
3 garlic cloves
4 tsp chilli oil, half for frying
   and half for dressing
2 sprigs of thyme
60g breadcrumbs
300g (1 block) silken tofu
2 tbsp gochujang paste (or
   tomato paste if you wanna lay
   off the heat)
5 tbsp nutritional yeast
2 tbsp dark soy sauce
salt and pepper

1. Bring a large saucepan of water to the boil and salt the water. Add the pasta and cook according to the packet instructions. It should take around 10 minutes for al dente. Chuck 2 of the garlic cloves into the boiling water (don't worry this isn't a typo, it makes the cloves less bitter and will go in our sauce later).

2. Meanwhile, heat 2 teaspoons of the chilli oil in a large frying pan on a medium heat and fry the remaining clove of garlic (left whole) and the sprigs of thyme until golden and crispy. Then throw the breadcrumbs into the pan (don't actually throw them, it's just an expression), season them and fry for 3–5 minutes until toasted. Remove the breadcrumbs and pop them in a bowl for the end.

3. Now for the final bit of kit. Take a food processor and blitz the silken tofu, gochujang, nutritional yeast and soy sauce until smooth. Fish out the two garlic cloves from the boiling water and add them to the food processor, blitzing once more.

4. Take some pasta water out using a mug (around 100ml) and drain the linguine. Pop the creamy chilli sauce into the now-empty frying pan and pour in the reserved pasta cooking water. You might only need half to three-quarters of the sauce, depending on your pasta. Mix until you have a smooth and silky sauce, then lower the linguine into the sauce and stir together.

5. Top with the chilli oil, 2 pinches of the garlicky breadcrumbs (save the rest for other pasta dishes that need a kick) and devour. You can serve this one directly in the pan or into bowls if you want to divide the portions up evenly, I guess.

Quick Eats

CALS: 842 | **PROTEIN:** 41g | **FAT:** 16g | **SAT FAT:** 2.3g | **CARBS:** 126g | **SUGAR:** 17g | **SALT:** 4.1g | **FIBRE:** 13g

ONE-POT MESSY VEG & RICE

In a pan, quick as you can.

What is the thinking behind this? I'll be wholly honest, this is essentially me wanting to shove a load of veggies onto your plate, but have it taste wonderful. This does just that. It's one of those meals that is what it is. No prim and proper presentation, just great veggies, all merged into one big pot, a bit like the Royal Variety Performance.

*7 mins prep + 13 mins cooking = **20 mins total***

SERVES 2

Quick Eats

1 red pepper
4 spring onions
1 courgette
light olive oil, for frying
2 garlic cloves
250g cherry tomatoes
1 tbsp tomato paste
2 tsp dried mixed herbs
pinch of dried chilli flakes, plus
   extra to serve if you like
15g fresh basil
1 x 250g pouch cooked
   wholegrain rice
150g cooked puy lentils
100ml water
½ lemon
salt and pepper

1. Dice up the pepper into little bite-sized pieces, discarding the core and seeds, and cut the spring onions and courgette into thin slices. Fry all of them in a large frying pan (or a large saucepan if your frying pan isn't deep enough) on a medium–high heat with a little bit of oil.

2. Peel then grate or dice the garlic into tiny pieces and get the tomatoes ready to go in too. Once the veggies in the pan have had a few minutes and begin softening, give it a season then add both the tomatoes and garlic.

3. When all the veggies are golden and softened, and the tomatoes have popped like the 5th November, this is a brilliant time to add the tomato paste, mixed herbs, chilli flakes and basil leaves. So do that. Let the spices become fragrant (aka you start to smell them a metre away from the pan) and the basil leaves wilt a bit, then add your cooked rice, puy lentils and water (this will help the rice steam up and go fluffy). If you have it, put a lid on your pan and turn the heat down to low.

4. Give the pan one final stir, a big old season with salt and pepper and a good squeeze of lemon juice. Top with a sprinkle more of the chilli flakes, if you like. Easy peasy. Serve it in bowls or straight out the pan. Get stuck in.

CALS: 426 | **PROTEIN:** 16g | **FAT:** 11g | **SAT FAT:** 1.9g | **CARBS:** 57g | **SUGAR:** 12g | **SALT:** 1.1g | **FIBRE:** 13g

PROPER PEASTO PASTA

The one you could make for your dad.

This is my go-to pesto recipe, and one I would love to humbly mark as the only pea pesto you should make. It is light, refreshing but also packed with protein. It's also tried and tested with success on national television by me, and TV never lies, so you know it's good.

*5 mins prep + 15 mins cooking = **20 mins total***

SERVES 3

100g frozen peas (no need to defrost)
100g breadcrumbs
30g fresh basil
15g fresh mint
5 sprigs of thyme
5 garlic cloves
1 lemon
1 tbsp apple cider vinegar
30g unsalted cashews
5 tbsp nutritional yeast
120ml extra virgin olive oil
50ml ice-cold water, plus extra for consistency if needed
200g linguine
salt and pepper

1. Put the following in a lovely big food processor: the peas, half the breadcrumbs, the basil stalks and leaves, the mint leaves, leaves from 3 of three sprigs of thyme, 2 of the garlic cloves, the juice from half the lemon, the vinegar, cashews, nutritional yeast and 6 tablespoons of the olive oil. Add the ice-cold water then blitz it all up.

2. You may need to add more water and maybe a bit more oil to get to a nice creamy and smooth consistency. Season to taste and use the juice from the other half of the lemon to balance everything up.

3. Boil water in a large saucepan, salt it, and cook your pasta for 9–11 minutes.

4. Grab a frying pan and put it on a low-medium heat. Chuck in 2 tablespoons of olive oil, then crush the remaining garlic cloves and chuck those in whole along with the remaining sprigs of thyme. Once they start getting fragrant, like 'oooh, that smells lovely' kind of fragrant, add the remaining breadcrumbs and toast for 3–5 minutes until golden and crispy, then remove from the pan and pop into a bowl for later.

5. Grab a mug of the pasta cooking water, then drain the pasta. Add the pesto and half the mug of reserved pasta cooking water to the pan, and mix until you have a sauce. Make sure it's lovely before adding the pasta in, then mix everything all together.

6. Finish with the breadcrumbs and a quick season.

7. Go enjoy it.

CALS: 875 | **PROTEIN:** 26g | **FAT:** 48g | **SAT FAT:** 7g | **CARBS:** 79g | **SUGAR:** 8.6g | **SALT:** 0.56g | **FIBRE:** 11g

PROPER EATS

3

LIGHT UP THE CANDLES, IT'S TIME FOR A PROPER MEAL

This chapter is full of the gamechanging meals

These dishes are the staples of mine for dinnertime and for when you want to make a showstopper of a meal, whether that's for a loved one, your mate or maybe a date.

In cooking, repetition and consistency are probably the best ways of acheiving something great. You didn't come here for a TED talk, but my point is you'll see that I repeat some of my core techniques and recipes, such as the 'cream' sauce made with silken tofu, and reinvent them. Like that sauce, you'll find that it only takes a few tweaks to transform some of the recipes you already know and love. So go and make a difference to the food that the people in your life enjoy! And make them something from here, please, I mean you may as well you've bought the book.

SWEET & STICKY TOFU

For those who think tofu is boring.

Hi, you might've stumbled on this page as the first recipe in the Proper Eats chapter and wondered, 'why is tofu the first recipe on here? It's bloody boring, sorry'. Well, for those who have this mindset, this recipe will change that, and I can say that confidently. Purely because thousands of others have tried my tofu and agree. Not to flex, but I'm flexing.

*8 mins prep + 12 mins cooking = **20 mins total***

SERVES 2

baking paper (not an ingredient but something you may have to go to the shops and get)
200g tenderstem broccoli
1 garlic clove
3 tbsp extra virgin olive oil
1 lemon
280g (1 block) extra-firm tofu
40g cornflour
light olive oil, for frying
3 tbsp light soy sauce
2 tbsp agave syrup
2 tbsp apple cider vinegar
1 tsp red miso paste
1 tsp tomato paste
20ml water
1 x 250g pouch cooked wholegrain rice
salt and pepper

To serve
1 spring onion
1 lime, cut into quarters
a pinch of sesame seeds

1. Whack your oven on to 200°C (fan 180°C/gas mark 6). Grab a baking tray, line it with baking paper and, on that, pop the tenderstem broccoli. Grate the garlic and mix it with the extra virgin olive oil in a small jug, then drizzle it over the broccoli. Cut the lemon in half and squeeze some juice over the broccoli. Season and whack in the oven for about 12 minutes.

2. Give the tofu a quick squeeze before chopping it into little cubes. Grab a bowl with a lid if you've got one (if not, any container with a lid works). Pop the cornflour in. Add a pinch each of salt and pepper before chucking in the tofu cubes. Close the bowl (or container) with the lid and shake to coat all of the pieces.

3. Heat a little bit of oil in a large frying pan on a medium heat, add the tofu and fry, making sure they all stay in one layer and don't stack on top of each other. Keep going for 6–8 minutes until all the sides are crisped up and golden.

4. Remember that small jug? Go rinse it and dry it out. Then add the soy sauce, agave syrup, vinegar, miso paste and tomato paste. Mix well, adding the water to help it go saucy.

5. Now, cut the green parts of the spring onion into thin slices and chop the lime into quarters ready for the end. Once the tofu's ready, reduce the heat to low, chuck the sauce into the pan and coat all the tofu so it's nice and sticky. At this point, your broccoli is ready. Turn off the oven and take it out. Not for a date.

6. Pop the rice into the microwave for 90 seconds at 900W or whatever your packet and machine says to do. Plate up. Rice first, then tofu on top or to the side, and broccoli definitely to the side. Sprinkle on the spring onion and serve with lime quarters for squeezing. Finish with some sesame seeds.

7. Eat it mate. That's it.

CALS: 696 | **PROTEIN:** 20g | **FAT:** 32g | **SAT FAT:** 5.1g | **CARBS:** 74g | **SUGAR:** 22g | **SALT:** 4.5g | **FIBRE:** 9.5g

CREAMY CHICKPEA CURRY

We all love a curry here. And this one's my take on your alternative to a korma, pasanda or any form of curry that just tickles the senses and doesn't blow your head off. I love it, you'll love it, Sheila down my road loves it, so enjoy it. I don't have anyone called Sheila down my road, but I bet if there was a Sheila, she'd enjoy the curry.

*5 mins prep + 15 mins cooking = **20 mins total***

SERVES 3—4

1 white onion
2 garlic cloves
3cm (1¼in) piece of ginger
drizzle of vegetable oil
2 tsp garam masala
2 tsp ground cumin
2 tsp ground turmeric
1 x 160g tin of coconut cream
200ml veggie stock
1 x 400g tin chickpeas
2 tbsp ground almonds
1 tbsp agave syrup
50g (handful of) baby spinach
salt and pepper

To serve
pinch of fresh coriander
1 lime
1 tsp flaked almonds
1 x 250g pouch cooked basmati
  rice
3–4 rotis (optional)

A mild and sensational curry.

1. Chop chop, my friend. Get the onion niced and diced, then peel and either dice or grate both the garlic and ginger. Heat the vegetable oil in a large frying pan on a medium heat, add the onion, garlic and ginger and fry everything together. A quick pinch of salt and pepper at this stage is key in my opinion.

2. Next up, once that's golden and softened, add the spices, the coconut cream and veggie stock and stir together. Let it bubble away while you drain the chickpeas in a colander, then chuck those into the mix as quick as you can, because this is a 20-minute vegan book and I don't want you wasting time on anything else apart from me.

3. Season the curry to taste, then add the ground almonds and agave syrup and cook for about 8 minutes until reduced and thickened.

4. At this point, get the finishing bits ready. I want that coriander nicely chopped and the lime cut in half by the time that curry is ready. Thank you.

5. Chuck the baby spinach into the pan and stir in until the spinach has literally turned into nothing (basically wilted), then sprinkle the flaked almonds and the coriander on top. At this point, pop the rice into the microwave for 90 seconds at 900W or whatever your packet and machine says to do.

6. Serve the curry in the pan with a good squeeze of lime juice on top and pop the rice onto your plate with a roti if you fancy it. Then eat, with your date ... maybe? I don't know.

CALS: 381 | **PROTEIN:** 9.8g | **FAT:** 20g | **SAT FAT:** 8.7g | **CARBS:** 37g | **SUGAR:** 7.6g | **SALT:** 0.24g | **FIBRE:** 6g

A KIND-OF CARBONARA

I've spent years perfecting a comforting, filling, plant-based carbonara, and this one's been tried and tested by not only my mum, but a hundred other people who ate it at a pop-up event I hosted in Borough Market in the summer of 2021. I say this like I'm reflecting on past memories, but my goodness it was a great one.

*7 mins prep + 13 mins cooking = **20 mins total***

SERVES 2

200g tagliatelle, or another
  type of pasta
200g block of tempeh
light olive oil, for frying
4 tbsp dark soy sauce
1 tsp sweet smoked paprika
1 tbsp agave syrup

For the sauce
150g (about ½ block) silken tofu
100ml oat milk
30g (handful of) unsalted
  cashews
5 tbsp nutritional yeast
1 tsp Dijon mustard
2 garlic cloves

1. Boil water and add your pasta to the water. Cook according to your pasta's packet instructions. This doesn't really need a step but please do it. Salt your water too so it tastes like Nemo's home.

2. Cut the tempeh into tiny strips, so it resembles bacon lardons, and fry that in a frying pan with oil on a medium heat for a couple of minutes until it goes crispy. Once crispy, add the soy sauce, paprika and, finally, the agave syrup. Reduce the heat to low and cook the strips for about 3–4 minutes until they go slightly sticky.

3. Blitz your sauce using a food processor. That's the silken tofu, oat milk, cashews, nutritional yeast, mustard and garlic for the record. Once the sauce is smooth, set it aside until the pasta's done. Also, grab a half mugful of pasta cooking water and keep it to the side for the end.

4. Take a few 'bacon' bits out (that's for later), drain the pasta and put back into the saucepan on a medium heat with most of the bacon bits. Stir in the sauce gradually, chuck in the reserved pasta cooking water and mix it all up to make the magic happen.

5. Top with the remaining bacon bits and devour on sight, out of the pan.

A classic Italian dish, made by a British bloke.

CALS: 907 | **PROTEIN:** 56g | **FAT:** 26g | **SAT FAT:** 3.2g | **CARBS:** 101g | **SUGAR:** 24g | **SALT:** 5.6g | **FIBRE:** 22g

Did you know that pasta is a universal love language? According to a study by Calum Harris.

BENNY BÁNH MÌ

I've met loads of people who have come from completely different walks of life, and all have had different experiences with food. Ben is someone I met via social media, and while he probably likes my cooking, he is also very hard to please. You'd be more satisfied with a thumbs up from him than a Michelin star. So, when it comes to making a sandwich, there is only one that will satisfy Ben: the bánh mì. Hailing from Vietnam, it's a brilliant baguette that mixes freshness with nuttiness, and all-in-all just hits incredibly well. So please, do me a favour and bánh mì from making this.

*10 mins prep + 10 mins cooking = **20 mins total***

SERVES 2

280g (1 block) extra-firm tofu
2 tbsp light olive oil

For the pickled vegetables
½ medium carrot
½ cucumber
100ml apple cider vinegar (or rice wine vinegar)
1 tbsp agave syrup
big pinch of salt

For the glaze
4 tbsp light soy sauce
1 tsp sriracha sauce, plus extra for drizzling
1 tbsp rice wine vinegar
1 tsp agave syrup

To finish
1 baguette
1 tbsp smooth peanut butter
vegan mayo (optional)
fresh coriander
1 lime

1. Pickly pickle time. Using a potato peeler, peel the carrot and cucumber into ribbons then pop into a bowl or a container that has a lid with the vinegar, agave syrup and salt. Leave it in the fridge to pickle up.

2. Drain the tofu and chop it up into thick but small slices. Basically, chop the block in half lengthways and then chop those halves into slices.

3. Heat the oil in a large frying pan on a medium-high heat. Once hot, add the tofu slices and fry for 2–3 minutes on each side. In a small jug, mix the glaze ingredients together forever. Once the tofu is golden and crispy, pour the glaze mix over the top and fry for about 2 minutes until sticky and everything's coated. Take it off the heat once you've done this.

4. Now slice the baguette in half and open it up like an oyster opening up to show you its pearl. Toast it if you like, but then once that's done, let's serve, shall we?

5. Add the peanut butter and some vegan mayo (if you're using it) to the bottom of the baguette then add the crispy tofu. Place the pickled veg on top and drizzle with more sriracha and vegan mayo (if you like). Finish with a sprinkle of fresh coriander and a squeeze of lime juice.

6. Slice in half, eat it, and if you see Ben Rebuck in the London or Hertfordshire area, say 'thank you' to him for no apparent reason.

CALS: 644 | **PROTEIN:** 21g | **FAT:** 35g | **SAT FAT:** 5g | **CARBS:** 57g | **SUGAR:** 17g | **SALT:** 6.4g | **FIBRE:** 7.3g

BUTTER 'CHICKEN' (WELL ACTUALLY TOFU) CURRY

My mates love this one.

This is similar to the classic Indian dish, butter chicken, but quicker to make, using tofu instead of chicken, and it's one of those dishes that needs to be enjoyed by many. It's a super-filling, super-satisfying showstopper that'll remain in your cooking repertoire for a good few years, until I come up with another recipe.

*5 mins prep + 15 mins cooking = **20 mins total***

SERVES 2

1 onion
4 garlic cloves
3cm (1¼in) piece of ginger
½ red chilli, deseeded (or the whole chilli if you like heat)
light olive oil, for frying
280g (1 block) extra-firm tofu
40g cornflour
2 tsp smoked paprika
3 tsp ground cumin
3 tsp garam masala
500ml passata
1 x 160g tin of coconut cream
3 tbsp vegan butter
100ml hot water (optional)
salt and pepper

To serve
handful of fresh mint (optional)
handful of fresh coriander
1 x 250g pouch cooked basmati rice (optional)
½ lime
a few poppadoms (optional)
mango chutney (optional)

1. Blitz the onion, garlic, ginger and chilli in a food processor until smooth.

2. Heat some oil in a large saucepan on a medium heat, add the onion, garlic, ginger and chilli mixture and fry for about 5–7 minutes until everything is golden.

3. Meanwhile, tear the tofu into pieces with your bare hands and make sure they're uneven and bite-sized, almost chicken-y. Pop the cornflour in a bowl with a lid, season it with salt and pepper, then chuck in the tofu pieces, close the lid and shake it up.

4. Heat a little oil in a large frying pan on a medium-high heat, chuck in that tofu and fry for about 5–7 minutes until the pieces go extra crispy on all their sides.

5. When the onion-y chilli garlic-y paste is cooked, season it, then add the spices. Once the spices go fragrant, and you'll know when, pour in the passata and coconut cream and stir in the butter. If there's still some coconut cream on the sides of the tin, spoon it into a small bowl and save it for the end. Season with salt and pepper and then let that bubble away until thickened on a medium heat.

6. At this point, you may be waiting for things to be done, so I'd go ahead and chop the mint (if using) and coriander for the finishing bit. If you scrunch the herbs into a tight ball, then thinly slice from one end of the ball to the other you end up with lovely diced herbs in no time at all.

Continued...

CALS: 913 | **PROTEIN:** 24g | **FAT:** 48g | **SAT FAT:** 21g | **CARBS:** 85g | **SUGAR:** 21g | **SALT:** 1.7g | **FIBRE:** 11g

7. Once the tofu is cooked and crispy, chuck that into the curry sauce and stir until the tofu is coated – you should be left with a delicious-looking curry. This process should take 3 or so minutes, but you can add the 100ml hot water, turn the heat down and let it reduce for longer if you're waiting for your mates to arrive. You'll know when it's the right consistency when it looks like the photo.

8. Pop the rice (if using) into the microwave for 90 seconds at 900W or whatever your packet and machine says to do.

9. Serve it with a squeeze of lime and the chopped herbs. Drizzle that with the leftover coconut cream from earlier (if there's any) and give it a final season for good luck. Then just eat with the cooked rice and/or poppadoms, with a side of mango chutney if you fancy it. Happy? You should be.

TOP TIP:

You can stick the tofu pieces in the oven instead of frying. It does take longer but you end up with super-crispy pieces. If that's what you'd like to do, ignore step 4, and add the tofu to a baking tray lined with baking paper, drizzle with oil, and cook for 20 minutes at 200°C (fan 180°C/gas mark 6).

CHERRY TOMATO RIGATONI

Tomato pasta is a staple dish for every British and Italian person ever. And there's nothing better than making your own tomato pasta with the humble cherry tomato. I mean, they might not be humble, but they're tiny so can't have that much ego to be honest. One thing I wanted to do with my tomato pasta was not only make it taste great, but also give you a good amount of protein without taking away from the classic. I think this might be the dish in this book that people make the most, and one for your mates, and your family.

*6 mins prep + 14 mins cooking = **20 mins total***

SERVES 2

200g rigatoni
1 white onion
olive oil, for frying
2 large or 3 medium garlic cloves
250g cherry tomatoes on the vine
3 tbsp apple cider vinegar
3 tbsp tomato paste
150g (about ½ block) silken tofu
4 tbsp nutritional yeast
salt and pepper
fresh basil, to serve (optional)
The Parmigiano Alternativo (see page 212, optional)

1. Ah, the obvious bit. Cook the pasta in salted boiling water. Follow the packet instructions but it should take about 12 minutes.

2. Chop up the onion until finely diced, then fry in a large frying pan with a drizzle of olive oil on a medium heat.

3. Take the skins off the garlic and chop the cloves in half. You only want the essence of garlic in this recipe, however I won't judge you if you want to grate them and have it merge into the sauce. Strip the tomatoes off the vine and cut each tomato in half. Once the onions have softened, give them a season and chuck in the garlic and tomatoes. Fry for about 6–8 minutes until the tomatoes have broken down, then add the vinegar and tomato paste and let that reduce fully.

4. In a food processor, blitz up the silken tofu and nutritional yeast together until smooth. Or, if you have spare from any of the previous recipes where you've done this step, go grab it.

5. We're getting to the end, don't worry. In the large frying pan you should have a rich tomato sauce that's thick, and needing a bit more love and attention. Fish out the garlic cloves from the sauce using a spoon (unless you've grated them).

6. Grab a mugful of pasta cooking water, then drain the cooked rigatoni. Pour about 70ml of the reserved pasta cooking water (half the mug) into the tomato pan, along with the silken tofu cream. Stir until fully combined and silky, then chuck in the rigatoni.

7. Stir until the pasta is looking creamy and tomatoey – just like the photo. Top with a sprig of basil to make it look fancy (optional), salt and pepper it up, top with my Parmigiano Alternativo, if you like, and eat.

CALS: 715 | **PROTEIN:** 36g | **FAT:** 19g | **SAT FAT:** 2.3g | **CARBS:** 90g | **SUGAR:** 20g | **SALT:** 0.49g | **FIBRE:** 16g

SMOKY BARZ CHILLI

Back in 2019, when I first started writing recipes, I would directly message every cook and public figure to get them to notice what I was doing, and hopefully show their love. One day, I posted a recipe for this chilli and sent it around. Only one person got back to me, and that was none other than Jamal Edwards. Jamal bigged it up online, shared it on his socials, and to me, that was life changing. He was the first person of major influence to do that. Afterwards, he kept supporting what I was doing - he'd put me forward for things to level my career up, at no benefit to him. Jamal is no longer with us, however, his influence lives on within what I do and for many others. There's no other person that deserves a recipe devoted to them as much as him. Enjoy the Smoky Barz Chilli.

*6 mins prep + 14 mins cooking = **20 mins total***

SERVES 3—4

5 spring onions
2 garlic cloves
2 tbsp light olive oil
1 x 400g tin chickpeas
1 x 400g tin black beans
1 tsp each smoked paprika, ground cumin, chilli powder (mild or medium works)
1 tsp fennel seeds (optional)
1 tsp ground cinnamon
1 tsp dried mixed herbs
1 tsp chipotle paste
1 tbsp tomato paste
1 x 400g tin chopped tomatoes
200ml boiling water
2 tbsp light soy sauce
1 tbsp balsamic vinegar
salt and pepper

To serve
handful of fresh coriander
1 lime
1 x 250g pouch cooked wholegrain rice
Tabasco, to taste (optional)
handful of tortilla chips (optional)

1. Finely chop up the spring onions and garlic. Heat the olive oil in a large saucepan on a medium–high heat and add the spring onions and garlic. Give it a season as well and let that all soften.

2. Drain the chickpeas and black beans using a colander and leave them to one side (don't worry, they're coming back in a bit). Now chuck the spices, dried mixed herbs and the chipotle and tomato pastes into the pan, stir it all up, and when it becomes fragrant (or when your kitchen smells of spices), add in those chickpeas and beans.

3. Pour in the chopped tomatoes and the rest of the ingredients except for the rice and coriander obviously. Let it bubble away for a good 10 minutes or until everything's nice and reduced. Give it a good season with salt and pepper and try it. Like it? Great.

4. While that's cooking, chop up the coriander and cut the lime in half. Also, pop the rice into the microwave for 90 seconds at 900W or whatever your packet and machine says to do.

5. Serve your chilli straight from the pan into bowls with the rice and top it with the lime juice and coriander. If you fancy some Tabasco and tortilla chips, add some, but that's about it, mate.

6. Devour.

CALS: 449 | **PROTEIN:** 18g | **FAT:** 14g | **SAT FAT:** 2g | **CARBS:** 53g | **SUGAR:** 15g | **SALT:** 2.8g | **FIBRE:** 16g

JACKFRUIT CHIPOTLE BURRITOS

They're spiced up and beanie.

A beanie burrito is something I think most vegans find themselves making when they fancy a quick burrito. This is also an ode to my cousin Sam, who trademarked these as the 'Triple Bs' – banging beanie burritos. One for when you're super hungry.

*8 mins prep + 12 mins cooking = **20 mins total***

SERVES 2

4 spring onions
2 garlic cloves
2 tbsp light olive oil, for frying
1 x 400g tin black beans
1 x 400g tin jackfruit
1 tsp ground cumin
1 tsp smoked paprika
2 tsp chipotle paste
3 tbsp agave syrup
2 tbsp tomato paste
1 ripe avocado
5g fresh coriander
1 lime
1 x 250g pouch cooked
   wholegrain rice
2 wholemeal tortilla wraps
salt and pepper

To serve
hot sauce
Jalapeño & Grape Salsa (page 217, optional)
vegan yogurt (optional)

1. Chop up the spring onions and garlic into thin slices, and keep back the green parts of the spring onion for the end. Then fry them in light olive oil in a large frying pan for 3–4 minutes until softened. Salt and pepper these.

2. At this point, rinse and drain the black beans and jackfruit in a colander, and chuck those in the frying pan along with the ground spices.

3. In a small jug, mix the chipotle paste, agave syrup and tomato paste together with a splash of hot water until you have a lush chipotle sauce. Pour that into the beans and jackfruit mixture and let it bubble away until thickened. Whack the heat down to low once that's happened.

4. Peel and stone the avocado then mash it in a large bowl with the coriander. Slice your lime in half then squeeze half the lime juice into the bowl and mix it all together with a pinch of salt.

5. Pop the rice into the microwave for 90 seconds at 900W or whatever your packet and machine says to do.

6. While that's happening, you can start assembling. Pop the following in the bottom middle of the wrap and make sure not to overstuff it: mashed avo first, then the beans and jackfruit, then the rice. Finish with a splash of hot sauce, the green slices of spring onion, a squeeze of the other half of lime or, if you fancy it, my Jalapeño & Grape Salsa, or some vegan yogurt.

7. Wrap it up as tight as possible, mate, and then toast the bottom in a large frying pan so it's sealed up. Slice in half and eat. Or just look at it, or better yet, wrap it up in foil, stick it in the fridge and eat the next day.

CALS: 1017 | **PROTEIN:** 27g | **FAT:** 38g | **SAT FAT:** 7.1g | **CARBS:** 125g | **SUGAR:** 35g | **SALT:** 4.2g | **FIBRE:** 29g

TEMPEH SMASH BURGERS

Because we all deserve a treat.

I love burgers, but it's hard to have a burger recipe in here that's not just 'meat-free burger', with 'vegan cheese', and 'vegan veganing alternatives'. So, here's my burger, one that's different from what you're used to, and one that you'll go away from at the end of this recipe thinking, 'THAT WAS ACTUALLY A BANGING BURGER'. It's all in the burger sauce. Also, there is not a recipe for chips in here, but there is a video on my Instagram page on how to make the best chips as a compromise. There is a lot going on here, so once you finish with the patties, put stuff away, clean the board, then crack on with the rest of the recipe.

*13 mins prep + 7 mins cooking = **20 mins total***

MAKES 6 BURGERS

For the burger patties
3 tbsp flaxseed
6 tbsp lukewarm water
100ml boiling water
60g raw couscous
3 spring onions, white parts only
3 garlic cloves
1 x 200g block of tempeh
2 tsp smoked paprika
3 tbsp tomato paste
1 tsp gochujang (optional)
40g panko breadcrumbs
3 tbsp dark soy sauce
1 tsp red miso paste
olive oil, for frying

For the burger sauce
1 pickled gherkin
5 chives

Continued on next page...

1. The bit you should do before starting the whole recipe: combine the flaxseed with the water in a bowl and let it sit for 5–10 minutes until it goes gloopy. That, my friend, is your vegan alternative to an egg. At the same time, pour the boiling water over the couscous in a heatproof bowl and cover the top with a plate. That should cook the couscous within 5 minutes.

2. Chop up the spring onions and garlic cloves into tiny pieces and pop in a large mixing bowl. Crumble in the tempeh, cooked couscous, flaxseed 'egg', and basically all the other patty ingredients (except the oil for frying). Use a potato masher to help break everything down, or even your bare hands will work.

3. Shape the mix into six burger patties using your hands – you'll end up with them quite thick (if they're too thin, they might break apart).

4. Store in the fridge until you're ready to fry, and in the meantime, make the sauce. Dice up the pickle and chives. Shove into a small bowl with the yogurt, tomato paste or ketchup, and onion chutney and season to taste.

Continued...

CALS: 428 | **PROTEIN:** 21g | **FAT:** 21g | **SAT FAT:** 2g | **CARBS:** 35g | **SUGAR:** 6.8g | **SALT:** 2.4g | **FIBRE:** 8g

3 tbsp vegan Greek-style
  yogurt
1 tbsp tomato paste or ketchup
1 tsp onion chutney
salt and pepper

**For the rest of the bits to make
it an actual burger**
1 beef tomato
1 pickled gherkin
6 white baps or burger buns
  (always check the label to
  make sure there's no milk or
  egg in there)
1 little gem lettuce
6 slices of vegan cheese
  (optional)

Yes, that's it.

5. Now's a good time to slice the tomato into thin discs, the other pickled gherkin into discs, the buns in half and the lettuce into thin strips.

6. Fry the burgers in a large frying pan with a drizzle of olive oil on a medium-high heat for 2 minutes on each side, carefully flipping them over halfway.

7. If you want to add vegan cheese, add a slice to the top of each burger and chuck in a splash of water into the pan to the side of the burgers. This will guarantee the cheese to melt.

8 When the burgers are frying on the second side, toast your buns in the same frying pan (if there's room, of course). Serve up the burgers in any order you like, but in my opinion, the best order is: bottom bun, burger sauce, lettuce, tomato, burger patty, more burger sauce, pickles, top bun.

9. Devour. Sorry I didn't do sides, forgive me please.

TOP TIP:

You can freeze the
uncooked patties for a
good month, or keep them
in the fridge for up to
3-4 days. You can also
use vegan mayo instead
of vegan yogurt should
you so wish.

THE ULTIMATE QUICK BOLOGNESE

This is not a Bolognese.

I have to say this before the traditionalists come after me. A Bolognese, for me, is one dish that I love, a meal that every family turns to, and a great one that can really stay with you for years to come. One that requires time to prepare and cook. But what if you don't have time? Well this Bolognese, or as I like to call it, Linguine Notabolognese, will hopefully give you the Bolognese feeling but quicker, and vegan.

*6 mins prep + 14 mins cooking = **20 mins total***

SERVES 2

5 spring onions (white parts only)
1 medium carrot
3 garlic cloves
light olive oil, for frying
120g shiitake mushrooms
120g chestnut mushrooms
200g linguine
1 tsp smoked paprika
2 tsp mixed herbs
4 tbsp tomato paste
200ml veggie stock, boiling hot please (½ stock cube dissolved in 200ml boiling water – or double up both if you are cooking ahead and have time to let it reduce completely)
150g cooked Puy lentils
3 tbsp balsamic vinegar
2 tbsp dark soy sauce
fresh basil, to serve
The Parmigiano Alternativo (see page 212), to serve
salt and pepper

1. Boil around 2 litres of water in a big saucepan and salt it so it tastes like the sea. For those who asked, 2 pinches of salt.

2. Chop up the spring onions into thin slices, and peel the carrot and garlic cloves. Grate the carrot on the side of the box grater with bigger holes, and the garlic cloves on the side of the box grater with the smaller holes. Pop those all in a large frying pan with a drizzle of olive oil and a pinch of salt and pepper. Fry on a medium-high heat.

3. While that's got a head start, chop up your mushrooms into nice little cubes, and chuck those in the same pan as the onions, garlic and carrot. Get another pinch of salt and pepper in and fry for 6–8 minutes until the mushrooms have cooked through and are starting to crisp.

4. Pasta time. Add the linguine (or pasta of your choice, any will work babe) into the saucepan of boiling water and cook according to the packet instructions.

5. Add the paprika and herbs into the frying pan and mix everything properly together. Pop the tomato paste into the boiling hot stock and mix well together, and you should end up with a makeshift passata. Pour that all into the frying pan and immediately add the lentils, balsamic and soy sauce. Let it bubble away until it's all reduced, looking lovely and tomatoey.

6. When your pasta is cooked, drain it, and add it back into the saucepan. Then pop in two big ladles of sauce to the pasta and mix well. Serve in two bowls with extra sauce on top. Tear some fresh basil leaves and sprinkle over some of my Parmigiano Alternativo and devour it, love.

CALS: 779 | **PROTEIN:** 34g | **FAT:** 18g | **SAT FAT:** 2.1g | **CARBS:** 109g | **SUGAR:** 24g | **SALT:** 5g | **FIBRE:** 21g

MAC & 'CHEESE'

A guilty pleasure that isn't as guilty as you think. I'm sure everyone under the sun has a recipe for a macaroni and cheese, vegan or not. And this one, if you've made some of my pasta recipes before, won't come as a surprise. You might even go, 'Oh, it's just that'. But let me tell you, it's very very scrumptious. Also, cheesy. Like me at a karaoke bar.

*4 mins prep + 16 mins cooking = **20 mins total***

SERVES 2

250g macaroni
150g tenderstem broccoli
150g (about ½ block) silken tofu
100ml oat milk
50g unsalted cashews
1 tsp white miso paste
1 tsp Dijon mustard
4 tbsp nutritional yeast
light olive oil, for frying
50g breadcrumbs
2 garlic cloves
2 tsp dried mixed herbs
salt and pepper

A hit with the Mrs, if I had one.

1. Season a big old saucepan of boiling water with a pinch of salt and chuck in your macaroni. Keep stirring every so often while it cooks, as macaroni has tendency to stick together and clump. Chop the broccoli in half and add it to the boiling water 3 minutes after you added the macaroni. The macaroni will cook in 10 minutes, and the broccoli will cook in 7 minutes.

2. While the pasta is cooking, blitz up the tofu, milk, cashews, miso paste, mustard and nutritional yeast together in your trusted food processor until it makes a smooth cheesy sauce. Season it to taste please.

3. Okay, now for the finishing touch, but it's worth it. Add a drizzle of oil to a large frying pan over a medium heat. Put the breadcrumbs in and add the whole garlic cloves and dried herbs, with a pinch each of salt and pepper and fry for 3–5 minutes until golden and crispy.

4. Whack your grill setting on in the oven at the highest heat possible.

5. Assemble the avengers. Love a pun midway through a recipe. Get a little bit of pasta cooking water in a mug, then drain both the broccoli and macaroni in a colander. Grab a big baking dish and mix the mac and broc with three-quarters of the cheesy sauce and a little pasta cooking water until you get a lovely cheesy dish of mac and cheese. Boom. Drizzle the top with the remaining quarter of sauce, then chuck those crumbs on top of the macaroni and 'not cheese'. Grill in the oven for 4 minutes until the top is nice and crispy.

6. Carefully get the dish out the oven and serve on sight. Ideally spoon it into bowls. And enjoy.

CALS: 918 | **PROTEIN:** 42g | **FAT:** 26g | **SAT FAT:** 4.3g | **CARBS:** 120g | **SUGAR:** 14g | **SALT:** 1.2g | **FIBRE:** 16g

MISO GREENS & GNOCCHI

gnoch, gnoch, who's there?

I have to apologise but the jokes aren't going to stop. This dish - strangely - isn't like a gnocchi you've had before. Gnocchi is the lovechild of potatoes and pasta, and this miso butter sauce gives gnocchi a new lease of life, like a vintage denim jacket in an overpriced shop in London. I think this one's what I'd call your 'staple recipe'.

*6 mins prep + 14 mins cooking = **20 mins total***

SERVES 2

4 spring onions
3 garlic cloves
150g tenderstem broccoli
light olive oil, for frying
1 tbsp red miso paste
1 tbsp agave syrup
1 lemon, zest and juice please
80g frozen edamame beans (or garden peas)
150ml boiling water
2 tbsp tahini
2 tbsp extra virgin olive oil
250g gnocchi di patate (basically, potato gnocchi that's already prepared)
5g fresh tarragon (if you can't get it, Thai basil works great)
salt and pepper

1. First things first, get two frying pans out: one for the gnocchi and the other for the sauce. We're gonna start with the sauce first.

2. Chop up the white part of the spring onions into slices, and finely dice the garlic and broccoli. Add a drizzle of oil into one of the frying pans, then fry all the veg you've just chopped (putting the green spring onion bits aside for later) on a medium heat.

3. Once the veg has softened and is starting to crisp up, chuck in the miso paste, the agave syrup, half the lemon juice and zest and the edamame or peas. Give it a stir to make sure everything's come together, then season with salt and a touch of pepper. Reduce the heat, add the boiling water and tahini, stir until the tahini combines properly with the water, and let it bubble away on the lower heat until thickened.

4. Now to the second pan. Stick it on a medium heat and pour in the extra virgin olive oil. Gently put the gnocchi in the oil and fry for 3 minutes, stirring every 30 seconds to make sure they cook evenly and none of the gnocchi sticks to the pan.

5. Once golden and toasted, pop the gnocchi into the thickened miso sauce and season to taste. You might need to add a splash of water if the sauce has become too thick.

6. Chop up the fresh tarragon and the green parts of the spring onion. Finish off with the zest and juice of the other half of the lemon, a few slices of the spring onion greens and a touch of tarragon. Tuck in.

CALS: 595 | **PROTEIN:** 20g | **FAT:** 33g | **SAT FAT:** 4.6g | **CARBS:** 50g | **SUGAR:** 12g | **SALT:** 2.3g | **FIBRE:** 9.6g

BOSSMAN'S MUSHROOM KEBABS

Take the kebab to your kitchen.

My mate Sam Jones (@nomeatdisco on socials) makes a banging mushroom shawarma. This is nothing like his recipe, but I wanted to mention his name in a book. This kebab came to me in a fever dream, after watching my mates get doner kebab on a night out while I was left with chips. Nothing wrong with chips, but if you want something that's going to blow your mind, then go for this.

*8 mins prep + 12 mins cooking = **20 mins total***

SERVES 2

2 garlic cloves
100g plant-based Greek-style yogurt
pinch of fresh mint leaves
1 lemon
2 tbsp extra virgin olive oil (optional)
240g shiitake mushrooms
150g (about ½ block) extra-firm tofu
1 red onion
light olive oil, for frying
1 cucumber
1 tsp agave syrup
50ml apple cider vinegar
1 tsp each ground cumin, smoked paprika, ground cinnamon and dried mixed herbs
2 tbsp dark soy sauce
1 tbsp tomato paste
salt and pepper

To serve
little gem lettuce
2 white fluffy pittas or flatbreads
1 tsp rose harissa (optional)

1. First, the garlicky yogurt sauce. Grate the garlic cloves using a box grater then add that to a medium bowl with the yogurt. Mix well. Chop up the mint roughly and cut the lemon in half, then add the mint and lemon juice to the yogurt. Add a pinch of salt and give it a taste, see if you like it. And also, check the consistency – it should be thinnish. If not, add the extra virgin olive oil and mix. Leave it in the fridge until the end.

2. Chop the mushrooms, tofu and onion into thin slices and add to a large frying pan on a high heat with a drizzle of oil. Season with salt and pepper, then use a weight such as another pan to press down the shrooms and tofu and cook for 8 minutes until all the liquid comes out of the mushrooms and you get a nice golden colour on everything.

3. Meanwhile, make a quick pickle. Slice the cucumber into thin rounds then add to a small bowl with the agave syrup, apple cider vinegar and a pinch of salt. Transfer to the fridge, then chop up the gem lettuce.

4. Give everything a rough mix in the pan then add the spices, dried herbs, soy sauce and tomato paste. Make sure everything's coated and do the pressing method once more for about 2–4 minutes until everything is cooked and you start to get a nice char on the shrooms, onion and tofu.

5. Warm up your pittas or flatbreads either in a clean frying pan, straight over the hob or by resting it on top of the toaster on the lowest setting, then let them cool a bit. Slice open (if you're using a pitta) and stuff with the garlicky yogurt sauce, the shrooms and tofu, lettuce and cucumber pickle. Add a drizzle of harissa, if you like, and you're done.

CALS: 633 | **PROTEIN:** 28g | **FAT:** 27g | **SAT FAT:** 3.8g | **CARBS:** 60g | **SUGAR:** 22g | **SALT:** 3.9g | **FIBRE:** 14g

CAL'S TOMATO SOUP

Proper grub.

A tomato soup. I'll say, loud and proud, this is my favourite variation of a soup. And it's one I believe all of you are going to absolutely adore. I don't want to oversell this, so I'll shut up and let's cook.

*5 mins prep + 15 mins cooking = **20 mins total***

SERVES 2

baking paper (not an ingredient but something you may have to go to the shops and get)
750g cherry or baby tomatoes (without the vine)
5 garlic cloves
extra virgin olive oil, for drizzling (and extra for the top, optional)
2 slices sourdough bread
1 tsp dried mixed herbs
150g (about ½ block) silken tofu
1 tbsp red miso paste
2 tbsp tomato paste
100ml veggie stock (around ¼ stock cube dissolved in 100ml boiling water)
salt and pepper

To serve
fresh basil (optional)
½ lemon

1. Oven. On. 200°C (fan 180°C/gas mark 6). Please. Thank you. Right, get the tomatoes on a baking tray lined with baking paper, then take the garlic cloves but don't peel them and shove them straight onto the tray. Season with salt and pepper, drizzle with a glug of extra virgin olive oil, and bop in the oven for 15 minutes.

2. Slice the bread into crouton-sized pieces. Chuck them on a smaller baking tray and drizzle with a little olive oil, sprinkle the dried mixed herbs all over and season with salt and pepper. Pop them in the same oven as the tomatoes for 10–12 minutes, depending on how toasted you like croutons.

3. At this point, you are just waiting around, which is rare for this book, so enjoy the 10 or so minutes you have to spare, read something, I don't know. Oh, I know! Add the silken tofu, miso paste, tomato paste and veggie stock to a food processor or jug blender (the bigger the better), ready for blitzing.

4. Okay, at this point, the tomatoes are done. Squeeze the garlic cloves out of their skins using an oven mitt. Pop them and the tomatoes into the processor or blender and blitz with everything else. You should have a thick, slightly creamy soup. It is also worth seasoning to your taste.

5. Now serve up. Pour the soup into nice bowls (you might have some left over) then add some croutons on top, tear some basil leaves over that if you like and finally, a tiny squeeze of lemon juice on the top. Drizzle with extra virgin olive oil, if you like. That's all my friend, enjoy my soup. It's good soup.

CALS: 471 | **PROTEIN:** 19g | **FAT:** 12g | **SAT FAT:** 1.9g | **CARBS:** 62g | **SUGAR:** 19g | **SALT:** 2.6g | **FIBRE:** 8g

PEA & MINT ORZO

Orzo is essentially pasta and rice's lovechild. And I am a big fan of it. It's not only a great flavour carrier but it also cooks well in stocks, as opposed to the regular standard boiling water and salt. This pea and mint orzo dish brings back the memories of my favourite soup, but merges them with my love of risotto. Lo and behold, a brilliant orzo. Also, a one-pot dish, so you know.

*5 mins prep + 15 mins cooking = **20 mins total***

SERVES 2

1 courgette
olive oil, for frying
4 spring onions (white parts only)
2 garlic cloves
200g orzo
700ml veggie stock (1½ stock cubes dissolved in 700ml boiling water)
100g frozen peas
15g (handful of) mint
1 lemon
1 heaped tbsp vegan Greek-style yogurt (optional – it helps make it creamier)
salt and pepper

1. Slice the courgette in half then chop it into 1cm-thick half moons and fry in a large saucepan with a little olive oil on a medium heat.

2. Next up, chop the spring onions and garlic until nice and small, then fry in that same saucepan, until golden.

3. Chuck the orzo into the saucepan, give it a quick stir with everything in there, then pour in the veggie stock. Now, orzo is a bit unpredictable – nothing wrong with that, but it does need your attention. For the next 10 minutes, I'd like you to keep stirring everything until the orzo's cooked and the liquid has fully reduced, making sure there's no orzo stuck to the bottom of the pan.

4. Once the orzo is cooked, stir in the frozen peas, then reduce the heat to stop the orzo from overcooking. Now chop up the mint and slice the lemon in half.

5. Stir in three-quarters of the mint and the vegan yogurt (if you're doing that step) until it's come together like The Beatles, then season to taste, and finish with the rest of the mint and a little squeeze of lemon.

6. Take a step to look at what you've done. I hope it's turned out well. And now, eat.

TOP TIP:

If you have some leftover silken tofu cheese sauce from my Mac & 'Cheese' (see page 137) you can use that instead of the yogurt!

CALS: 516 | **PROTEIN:** 21g | **FAT:** 11g | **SAT FAT:** 1.4g | **CARBS:** 81g | **SUGAR:** 5.6g | **SALT:** 3.5g | **FIBRE:** 6.3g

TOMATOEY CHICKPEA & BROCCOLI CURRY

Roasted veg in a curry is a great success.

This curry is an essential of mine; one that I go to when I fancy a curry with a bit of depth to it. The roasted broccoli in this is dreamy, and if you fancy it, you can do other vegetables. A comforting, showstopper curry? Yes, ma'am.

*8 mins prep + 17 mins cooking = **25 mins total** Slightly longer, but worth it!*

SERVES 2–3

200g tenderstem broccoli
6 tbsp olive oil, plus extra for
  frying
2 tsp each garam masala,
  ground cumin and fennel seeds
1 tsp ground turmeric
1 x 400g tin chickpeas
thumb-sized knob of ginger
5 garlic cloves (or 3 garlic
  cloves and a white onion if you
  don't want too much garlic)
1 tbsp tomato paste
1 tsp dried chilli flakes (if you
  like spice)
1 tbsp mango chutney (I use
  Geeta's), plus extra to serve
1 x 400g tin chopped tomatoes
1 x 160g tin of coconut cream
salt and pepper

To serve
½ lime
15g fresh coriander
pomegranate seeds
poppadoms (optional)
Raita, My Way (page 218,
  optional)
1 x 250g pouch cooked
  basmati rice

1. Preheat the oven to 200°C (fan 180°C/gas mark 6). First things first; the veg. Get the tenderstem broccoli roughly chopped up and pop it to one side. Grab a big old roasting tray and add the 6 tablespoons of olive oil, then chuck in all the spices. Mix it until it forms a lovely curry paste then throw in the broccoli and drained chickpeas. Massage them with the spices, give it a season with salt and pepper then roast for about 12 minutes, please. You can also go longer if you'd like, but make sure you don't burn the thing.

2. Next up, the saucy bit. Heat a drizzle of oil in a large saucepan on a medium heat. Peel and then grate the ginger and garlic onto a board, shove it into the pan and fry until softened, then add the tomato paste, chilli flakes (if using) and mango chutney. Let everything come together before adding the chopped tomatoes and coconut cream. Season it to taste, reduce until saucy, then lower the heat until the veg in the oven is ready.

3. Transfer the roasted veg into the saucepan of sauce and mix all together, crank up the heat and stir till you've got a nice thick sauce and the veg has been fully mixed in. Then take it off. Not you, the saucepan.

4. To finish off the curry and make it look fancy, squeeze over some lime juice, chop up then chuck coriander all over the place, and sprinkle over the pomegranate seeds. You can also crush some poppadoms over the top as well as drizzling with Raita, My Way (see page 218).

5. Oh, and finally, pop the rice into the microwave for 90 seconds at 900W or whatever your packet and machine says to do.

6. Just sit back, have a look at what your mates think of you, and enjoy their great company and a brilliant curry.

CALS: 1190 | **PROTEIN:** 27g | **FAT:** 74g | **SAT FAT:** 23g | **CARBS:** 94g | **SUGAR:** 32g | **SALT:** 2.3g | **FIBRE:** 17g

CRISPY CHILLI TOFU

This is a brilliant dish of mine, and a crowd favourite too (the recipe has over 1 million views, not to brag but I'm bragging about it). It's got a sweet chilli sauce, beautifully crisp tofu and will remind you of your favourite Chinese takeaway but you'll go, 'I can't believe that's vegan'. Well, I hope you will.

*6 mins prep + 14 mins cooking = **20 mins total***

SERVES 2

280g (1 block) extra-firm tofu
30g cornflour
1 tsp Chinese five-spice
1 tsp smoked paprika
2 tbsp light olive oil, plus extra
  for frying
1 red pepper
1 yellow pepper
1 red chilli
3 garlic cloves
2cm (¾in) piece of ginger
4 tbsp light soy sauce
2 tbsp sweet chilli sauce
1 tbsp agave syrup
2 tbsp apple cider vinegar
1 tbsp tomato paste
50ml hot water (optional)
salt and pepper

To serve
2 spring onions
pinch of sesame seeds

I would cuddle this one, if it didn't burn my mouth.

1. Give the tofu a quick squeeze then cut it into 1cm thin strips. Next up, grab a bowl with a lid (or a big container with a lid – personally I like to use a takeaway container) and pop the cornflour and ground spices in. Add a pinch each of salt and pepper then chuck in the tofu strips. Close the bowl or container with the lid and shake to coat all of the pieces.

2. Heat 2 tablespoons of oil in a large frying pan on a medium heat. Add the coated tofu strips and fry for 3 minutes on each side until golden and crispy. Once you've done that, pop them in another bowl and do what's known as 'setting aside'.

3. While the tofu is cooking, chop the peppers and the chilli into thin slices (discarding the seeds and core from the peppers if you don't like heat) and peel and grate the garlic and ginger.

4. Fry the peppers and chilli in the now empty frying pan with a drizzle of oil on a medium heat. Fry until those peppers have gone slightly softer, which is about 3 minutes of cooking.

5. Chuck the grated garlic and ginger into the mix. Now put the soy sauce, sweet chilli, agave syrup, apple cider vinegar and tomato paste into the pan and cook for 2–3 minutes until you have a bubbly sauce. If you need more liquid, add the hot water, which will stop things from reducing too quickly.

6. Finish off the recipe. Add the crispy tofu from earlier into the pan and mix until it's fully coated in lovely chilli sauce.

7. Thinly slice your spring onions and top the tofu with that and some sesame seeds. Serve directly from the pan, because you did, in fact, cook it. A side for this? Some rice, probably. Eat it.

CALS: 380 | **PROTEIN:** 15g | **FAT:** 11g | **SAT FAT:** 1.7g | **CARBS:** 51g | **SUGAR:** 32g | **SALT:** 5.4g | **FIBRE:** 7.5g

HOT BOY SUMMER NOODLES

I made these on an absolute whim last summer, and I've been making them ever since. They're easy, quick … fitting with the whole theme of the book isn't it? But above all, they're a hot meal that you'll wanna serve up in no time. Get cooking, good looking.

*5 mins prep + 10 mins cooking = **15 mins total***

SERVES 2

100g (½ block) tempeh
light olive oil, for frying
3 spring onions
1cm (½in) piece of ginger
1 tbsp dark soy sauce
1 tsp white miso paste
1 tbsp agave syrup
1 tsp Marmite
1 tbsp sesame oil
50ml hot water
50g frozen peas
300g ready-to-wok medium
  thread noodles

To serve
a pinch of sesame seeds
2 tsp crispy chilli oil

1. Chop up the tempeh into small cubes, then get a large frying pan on the heat – medium please. Add a little bit of oil, then chuck in the tempeh and fry until it's, you guessed it, golden.

2. Slice the entire bunch of spring onions thinly then add just the white parts to the pan.

3. Grate the ginger using the smallest holes in your box grater and pop into a small jug. Mix in the soy sauce, miso paste, agave syrup, Marmite, sesame oil and, finally, the hot water, until you have a lovely smooth sauce. Leave to one side.

4. Once the tempeh has fried, add the frozen peas and the ready-to-wok noodles, along with a splash of water. Cook for about a minute, then add about half of the sauce, and then the remaining sauce bit by bit. Turn down the heat and stir the noodles, tempeh and veg together until all they're coated up and looking darker. Take the pan off the heat.

5. Top the noodles with the green parts of the onions, remember them? Then sprinkle on some sesame seeds, and finally, a drizzle of some good crispy chilli oil.

6. Just say the word 'beautiful' as if you're from Essex.

Proper Eats

They're hot because of chilli oil and nothing else.

CALS: 555 | **PROTEIN:** 25g | **FAT:** 23g | **SAT FAT:** 3.1g | **CARBS:** 57g | **SUGAR:** 12g | **SALT:** 3g | **FIBRE:** 9.2g

TIKKA TOFU WRAPS

A delight of the night.

Right, so you might've gathered that I really like wraps. And I also like tofu. I personally think tofu gets a bad reputation. Yes, it's plain, yes, it's odd, yes, no one really knows what it is, but recipes like this will get you talking about it in a good way. The tikka marinade with the mangoey drizzle makes this, again, an absolute winner.

*8 mins prep + 10 mins cooking = **18 mins total***

SERVES 2

280g (1 block) extra-firm tofu
2 garlic cloves
2cm (¾in) piece of ginger
150g vegan Greek-style yogurt
3 tbsp shop-bought tikka paste
2 tbsp light olive oil
½ cucumber
2 tbsp mango chutney
1 tbsp pomegranate seeds
salt and pepper

To serve
2 small tortilla wraps
Raita, My Way (page 218)
fresh coriander

1. Do you have a grill in your oven? Fab, babe, stick it on a high heat. And line a baking tray with foil.

2. Tofu. Again. Let's make it simple. Drain it quickly and chop it into small cubes.

3. Grate the garlic cloves and ginger. Then, in a large bowl, add the yogurt, tikka paste, grated garlic cloves, olive oil and a good pinch each of salt and pepper. Mix in the tofu and make sure all the cubes are evenly coated, then add the cubes to the lined baking tray. Grill for 8 minutes, until the tofu is charred and looking gnarly (yes, that's an adjective).

4. While that's grilling, chop the cucumber into discs, then halve those discs and season them with salt. Leave them to one side, ideally your best side. Then, in another small bowl, mix the mango chutney and pomegranate together and that's it.

5. Now the tortillas. You can either heat them in a large frying pan on a high heat – 30 seconds each side – or heat them directly over the gas flame for half that time.

6. Take the tofu carefully out of the oven, and then serve. Wraps first, then some Raita (see page 218), then the tofu, and finally the mango and pomegranate chutney. Add some of the salted cucumber slices and some sprigs of fresh coriander and you're good to go. Eat. Now. Put the book down.

TOP TIPS:

Flatbreads work as an alternative to wraps. Another tip: if you don't have a grill in your oven, use a griddle pan and fry the tofu on the hob instead.

152

Proper Eats

CALS: 585 | **PROTEIN:** 25g | **FAT:** 30g | **SAT FAT:** 4.7g | **CARBS:** 47g | **SUGAR:** 22g | **SALT:** 3.9g | **FIBRE:** 9.9g

THE SALVADOR DHALI

Because Dali would love a Dahl.

There is no other reason for me calling this the Salvador Dhali other than the fact that dhal is in Dali. But in a world where I am continually making puns like a dad at a barbecue, I have decided this is going to be the name of this dish. It is essentially my version of a classic tarka dhal and one you can knock up in about 20 minutes. It's creamy, it is more filling than other recipes in here, but honestly, it's worth it, dhal-ing.

*5 mins prep + 15 mins cooking = **20 mins total***

SERVES 2

150g red split lentils, washed in a sieve before cooking
2 tbsp tomato paste
1 tsp ground turmeric
2 tsp garam masala
1 tsp ground cumin
500ml veggie stock (or 1 stock cube dissolved in 500ml boiling water)
1 banana shallot (or 2 baby shallots)
4 garlic cloves
3cm (1¼in) piece of ginger
light olive oil, for frying
1 x 160g tin of coconut cream
100ml hot water
salt and pepper

To serve
2 vegan naan breads (or you could use 1 x 250g pouch cooked basmati rice)
handful of fresh coriander
½ lime

1. Chop chop. Sorry, I don't mean to be rude, but we have 20 minutes not 20 hours. In a large saucepan, add the red lentils, the tomato paste, spices and the veggie stock and boil, then leave to bubble on a medium heat for 15 minutes.

2. Preheat your oven to 200°C (fan 180°C/gas mark 6). That's for the naans. If you're not having them, skip this step.

3. While that's going on, remove the skins from the shallot(s), garlic and ginger, and slice thinly. Heat a little bit of oil in a large frying pan on a medium heat and fry the shallots, garlic and ginger for 3–5 minutes until everything softens and that's going to be brilliant for later. Add a pinch each of salt and pepper to this pan once everything's cooked.

4. When the lentils are almost done, about 10 minutes in, add the coconut cream and hot water and let it bubble away. Season that dhal too please.

5. Heat up your naans however you see fit. I like sprinkling water on them then sticking them in the hot oven for 2–3 minutes, but it's up to you what you do.

6. Chop up the coriander and slice the lime into quarters. Then serve your dhal in bowls and top with the cooked shallots, ginger and garlic. Serve with either rice or the naans (or both if you fancy, why not carb up?). Sprinkle coriander on top, then a squeeze of a quarter of lime on each bowl of dhal.

7. Take step 7 to think about what you've done. And stir. I hope you love it.

CALS: 858 | **PROTEIN:** 31g | **FAT:** 32g | **SAT FAT:** 17g | **CARBS:** 107g | **SUGAR:** 11g | **SALT:** 3.6g | **FIBRE:** 9.5g

CRISPY BUFFALO TOFU TACOS

The tacos of dreams.

I love a good taco. And a quick one? Bit of me, babe. These buffalo tacos are spicy, a real delight to eat and a great way of getting people on board with proper, filling tacos.

*8 mins prep + 12 mins cooking = **20 mins total***

SERVES 2

1 head of red cabbage
2 limes
4 tbsp agave syrup
280g (1 block) extra-firm tofu
50g cornflour
1 tsp ground cumin
1 tsp smoked paprika
olive oil, for frying
2 tbsp sriracha or equivalent
  thick hot sauce
2 tbsp vegan butter
1 tbsp tomato paste
50ml hot water
6 small tortilla wraps
salt and pepper

To serve
Jalapeño & Grape Salsa
  (page 217, optional)
fresh coriander

TOP TIP:

If you want tiny taco shells like you get in restaurants, use a 20cm cookie cutter and cut the shapes out before you begin the recipe.

1. First, the slaw. Carefully split the red cabbage in half with a knife, then into quarters. Halve the limes. Grab a potato peeler and peel strands off the cabbage until you end up with one big handful of thin strands. Pop that in a bowl with the juice of 1 lime, 1 tablespoon of the agave syrup and a pinch of salt, toss to mix and leave in the fridge until the end.

2. Give the tofu a quick squeeze before chopping it into little blocks. Next up, grab a bowl or other container with a lid and pop the cornflour and ground spices in. Add a pinch each of salt and pepper then chuck in the tofu. Close the bowl with the lid and shake to coat all of the pieces.

3. Fry all the tofu pieces in a large frying pan on a medium heat with a drizzle of olive oil for 3–5 minutes until properly crispy.

4. In a small saucepan, combine the rest of the agave syrup with the sriracha, vegan butter and tomato paste and the hot water on a medium heat until it makes a sticky and spicy sauce. And guess what you do with that?

5. Pour the sticky, spicy sauce into a little jug and leave to one side.

6. Almost done. Toast up your tortillas using a frying pan on high heat for less than 30 seconds on each side. Alternatively, you can do this in half the time by cooking the tortillas directly over the gas flame using tongs, if you have a gas hob.

7. Serve everything up together, wrap down, tofu down, then pour that gorgeous sauce. Slaw on top of that, and maybe some Jalapeño & Grape Salsa (see page 217). And finally, serve with a squeeze of juice from the remaining lime halves, a pinch of coriander, and a smile.

CALS: 911 | **PROTEIN:** 21g | **FAT:** 31g | **SAT FAT:** 7.7g | **CARBS:** 129g | **SUGAR:** 45g | **SALT:** 2.8g | **FIBRE:** 14g

PUDS

4

THE SWEET ONES

Sweet like maple, because we don't have honey here.

What more can I say apart from these desserts are sensational? There's a good amount of variety in each of them. Some are 20 minutes total to make, others are 20 minutes to prep, all of them are beautiful. And sweet.

This might be my five-year-old self's favourite chapter. I was a chubby bubby when I was younger and if I told that kid that he'd be able to have a section of sweet treats that just so happen to be vegan, he'd probably roll on the floor. There are also some really simple desserts, and definitely nothing extraordinary in this section. Not like a Miso Banana Crumble or anything ...

MISO BANANA CRUMBLE

Everyone loves a crumble, well not everyone. Let me correct that. MOST people love a crumble, but what if I told you that the crumble … could be improved? Blasphemy you might say, well … yeah, it sort of is. But this twist on crumble is an essential for me, and the reason why when I say 'I'm making a crumble', people trust me with it. The umami hint that the miso gives is indescribable, so enough talking from me, lemme show you.

*8 mins prep + 12 mins cooking = **20 mins total***

SERVES 4

200g mixed nuts (unsalted please)
5 heaped tbsp vegan butter
6 tbsp agave syrup
1 heaped tbsp plain flour
pinch of sea salt
100g porridge oats
5 medium bananas
1 tsp white miso paste
2 tsp ground cinnamon
vegan ice cream or vegan yogurt, to serve

1. Rightio then. You see that oven yeah? Put it on, 200°C (fan 180°C/gas mark 6).

2. In a food processor (it's back again), blitz up the mixed nuts until you have a nice crumb.

3. In a big old mixing bowl, pop in the butter, half the agave syrup, the blitzed nuts, flour, pinch of sea salt and porridge oats, and mix together with your hands until completely combined. After that, wash your hands, obviously.

4. Now we need a deep baking dish, ideally around 20cm wide, yeah that one, grab it. Peel the bananas and slice them into rough chunks, then pop at the bottom of the dish. Mix together the miso paste with the rest of the agave syrup and the cinnamon, then stir it in with the bananas and use a fork to bash them around and mix. It is okay if the bananas break down – you essentially want them half mashed, half whole.

5. Spoon the crumble mix on top of the bananas and pack it down so there are no gaps. If you have spare crumble mix, good for you, store it or eat it on the spot. Then stick it in that hot oven for 12 minutes or until golden brown on top.

6. Take the crumble out the oven, once it's cooked obviously, you absolute–

7. Serve the crumble with a dollop of vegan ice cream or yogurt and serve for yourself, a loved one or your mates.

The classic, flipped on its head.

CALS: 781 | **PROTEIN:** 21g | **FAT:** 41g | **SAT FAT:** 7.6g | **CARBS:** 77g | **SUGAR:** 48g | **SALT:** 0.54g | **FIBRE:** 8.3g

ONE-PAN COOKIE

Honesty is the best policy in every relationship, which is why this dessert in my opinion borders on the healthy-ish side of the book. It's a real sweet treat, and one I'm genuinely sure everyone's going to love. I made this recipe up for my mate Emily, who basically said quote-unquote, 'that is stunning, m'dear'. So, naturally, it's got to go in my book. If you fall in love with this cookie, thank Emily. Two rules with this one: 1. Make sure your pan is oven-safe. And 2. Try not to indulge in it by yourself.

*8 mins prep + 17 mins cooking = **25 mins total** (slightly longer, I'm sorry)*

SERVES 2

70g coconut oil
160g self-raising flour
1 tsp ground cinnamon
pinch of salt
2 ripe bananas
90g dark chocolate (70% cocoa solids)
150ml maple syrup (yes, it's a lot, you can use agave syrup if you'd like)

To serve
2 tbsp coconut yogurt or vegan Greek-style yogurt
a few strawberries

1. Oven. Preheat. 180°C (fan 160°C/gas mark 4) this time.

2. Stick a large ovenproof frying pan on a medium heat and add the coconut oil. Once the coconut oil is melted, take it off the heat.

3. Let it cool for a minute or two, then add the flour, cinnamon and salt to the pan of cooled oil and stir well. Once that's combined, go peel the bananas and mash them up in a bowl until there are absolutely no lumps. And chop the chocolate into chunks.

4. Add the maple syrup to the pan, as well as the bananas and chocolate. Make sure everything is combined well, then stick the pan in the oven for 17 minutes to cook or until the top is golden brown. Also, if your pan has a rubber handle, wrap the handle in foil to protect it from melting in the oven. I learnt the hard way.

5. Once the cookie is looking gorgeous, gently take it out of the oven with oven mitts, then let it cool before drizzling with a spoonful of yogurt and some strawberries that I'd recommend halving or slicing.

6. Eat the damn cookie.

CALS: 1241 | **PROTEIN:** 14g | **FAT:** 65g | **SAT FAT:** 51g | **CARBS:** 144g | **SUGAR:** 76g | **SALT:** 0.95g | **FIBRE:** 11g

SOFT-BAKED CHOC & COFFEE COOKIES

Oooh, that's interesting, tell me more babe.

Cookies, come get your cookies, come get the cookies, cookies, cookies. Cookies. These cookies are so brilliant that I needed to say the word cookies 7 times. The espresso works perfectly in these, and trust me, this will be on the baking list for a great vegan cookie. They've got a great crispy edge but a soft middle. That's basically the definition of a perfect cookie.

*8 mins prep + 12 mins cooking = **20 mins***

MAKES 8 BIG TO 12 SMALL

170g vegan butter (I recommend Flora, Naturli or Stork for this)
1 tbsp almond butter
3 tbsp agave syrup
2 tsp vanilla extract
80ml strong coffee (espresso or instant coffee strength), warm
170g light brown sugar
200g spelt flour or plain flour
2 tbsp cocoa powder
2 tbsp cacao powder
1 tsp baking powder
½ tsp bicarbonate of soda
150g dark chocolate (70% cocoa solids or above)

TOP TIP:

If your batter is a little too wet for shaping into blobs at step 3, pop it in a freezerproof container and freeze it for 30 minutes then continue with the recipe.

1. Preheat the oven to 200°C (fan 180°C/gas mark 6) and line a baking tray with baking paper.

2. In a large mixing bowl, beat the vegan butter, almond butter, agave syrup, vanilla extract, coffee and sugar together with a balloon whisk until combined and almost like a sugary butter. Now add in all the dry bits including the flour, cocoa and cacao powders, baking powder and bicarbonate of soda. Using a silicone spatula or a wooden spoon, combine it all together.

3. Chop up the chocolate into tiny chips, add that into the cookie batter and mix well. At this point, the batter will look a little wet, almost cakey, but do not worry. Wet your hands with water and pat on a tea towel so they're still damp but not dry. Shape golf-ball-sized blobs for each cookie, and pop them onto your baking paper lined tray, then press down each blob with your thumb or a wet spoon so they're slightly flattened. Make sure there's loads of space between each cookie. Bake for 12 minutes.

4. They will look properly soft, but don't worry, let them cool completely, and after that, let the eating happen. They will keep for up to 4 days in an airtight container.

CALS: 483 | **PROTEIN:** 7.6g | **FAT:** 26g | **SAT FAT:** 9.6g | **CARBS:** 50g | **SUGAR:** 33g | **SALT:** 0.55g | **FIBRE:** 6.9g

SALTED ALMOND BUTTER MILLIONAIRES

If you're a fan of millionaires then I love you, because you'll be making these. The almond butter makes for a perfect alternative to the classic shortbread. These are also brilliant to make for the week ahead if you fancy a sweet treat, or let's say you've got Susan from next door coming round for afternoon tea.

*18 mins prep + a bit longer to set in the fridge = **longer than 20 mins in total, but less than 20 mins to make it** (forgive me)*

MAKES 8 SQUARES
(OR 12 MINI SQUARES)

8 medjool dates (without the stones)
50g walnuts
160g porridge oats
1 tbsp agave syrup
50ml plant milk (oat or soy works best)
180g dark chocolate (70% or above), broken into pieces
1 tbsp coconut oil
a jar of smooth almond butter (you can use peanut butter, or tahini)
sea salt

One to bring to the mothers' meetings.

1. Make space in your fridge. Thank me later.

2. In a food processor, blitz up the dates and walnuts together until they make a sort of paste. Put that into a large mixing bowl and add the oats, a pinch of sea salt and the agave syrup.

3. Warm up the plant milk either using a milk frother (I cook for a living, of course I have one for coffee) or the classic way using a hob or the microwave. Pour into the mixing bowl and combine everything together using a silicone spatula. You should end up with a mixture that has a flapjack-like consistency, and it shouldn't be too wet. If that happens, add more oats.

4. Now line a deep baking tray (around 20cm square) with baking paper (or use a silicone baking tray without the paper) and press the oat mix evenly into the bottom. Make sure everything's flat and even.

5. Melt the chocolate and coconut oil in either a pan on the hob or microwave, then pour over the top of the oat base. While the chocolate and coconut oil mixture is still melted, add a few tablespoon blobs of almond butter on top of the chocolate and swirl using a metal skewer to look like something on the *Bake Off* signature challenge.

6. Add a final pinch of sea salt on the top and whack it in the fridge for at least 1 hour, or the freezer for 30 minutes.

7. Take it out of the tray, chop it into squares and tuck in. You should get a comfortable 8 squares or 12 mini squares, depending on your cutting skills. They will keep for up to a week in an airtight container in the fridge.

CALS: 497 | **PROTEIN:** 10g | **FAT:** 30g | **SAT FAT:** 10g | **CARBS:** 42g | **SUGAR:** 25g | **SALT:** 0.33g | **FIBRE:** 9.4g

Do NOT eat
the chocolate

Seriously,
whatever you
do don't eat it

Ah the dessert's
done, and you
didn't eat the—

—oh for
goodness sake

ROASTED PISTACHIO & PINEAPPLE MEDLEY

I wanted a recipe that was genuinely easy. Something that's a general dessert to have on a day to day, but a bit more opulent. And so, one evening, when I was eating yogurt (plant-based, of course), I came up with this. Stewing the pineapples with cinnamon pimps them up to another level, and it's got freshness, zing, creaminess, crunchiness and other adjectives I can't think of right now. Enjoy.

*5 mins prep + 15 mins cooking = **20 mins total***

SERVES 2

baking paper (not an ingredient but something you may have to go out and get)
100g unsalted shelled pistachios
3 tbsp agave syrup
2 tbsp desiccated coconut
pinch of salt
200g pineapple fingers (or ½ pineapple)
2 tsp ground cinnamon
1 lime
200g vegan Greek-style yogurt

Essentially, posh pineapple yogurt bowls.

1. Whack the oven on at 180°C (fan 160°C/gas mark 4).

2. Line a baking tray with baking paper and pop the pistachios on top. Drizzle 2 tablespoons of the agave syrup over the top and all the desiccated coconut and mix well. Sprinkle with the salt and bang it in the oven for about 10 minutes or until the nuts are golden and caramelised but still green.

3. Meanwhile, chop the pineapple fingers into little chunks (or, if you're preparing a whole pineapple, peel and chop the pineapple into little chunks carefully and don't send for me if it takes you longer than 20 minutes). Put the chunks in a large frying pan on a medium heat. After about 5 minutes, when they're warm and starting to caramelise, add the remaining agave syrup and the cinnamon. Stir the pineapple up and let it bubble away for about 6–8 minutes until fully caramelised and the pieces look golden and cinnamony.

4. Now the lime. Grab it and zest it using the smallest hole on the box grater, and slice it in half ready for juicing. Split the yogurt into two bowls, squeeze a quarter of the lime juice into each bowl and stir.

5. When the pineapple chunks are looking sticky, it's ready. Squeeze some lime juice on top to keep its freshness. Pistachios? Oh yeah. Take them out the oven. If you'd like a crumbly consistency, which is nice, bash them up in a pestle and mortar when they're cooler. You don't have to, mate, but it's nice.

6. Finish off the recipe by assembling your own bowls, with the pineapple chunks, limey yogurt and the pistachio pieces. Sprinkle over the zest and eat up the best ... yogurt bowl you've ever had.

CALS: 587 | **PROTEIN:** 17g | **FAT:** 36g | **SAT FAT:** 8.6g | **CARBS:** 41g | **SUGAR:** 37g | **SALT:** 0.63g | **FIBRE:** 11g

MOSCONI'S TIRAMISU

Ciao bella. Back in 1926, my friend Andrew's great-great-grandmother would make tiramisu for her small town in Malta. Generations later, her great-great-grandson Andrew Mosconi would not take on her cooking skills and instead came to me on how to make a tiramisu. I wish all of the above was true, but it sounded more interesting than the actual origin of the dish you're about to make. Basically, my mates Andrew and Mitchell love tiramisu - I found this out when we went to Milan together - so I'm making a version for this quick 20-minute book. Arrivederci.

*15 mins prep + 2–3 hours to set in the fridge = **longer than 20 mins***

SERVES 4

200ml brewed coffee (you can use instant coffee or a double espresso with boiling water)
300g (1 block) silken tofu
½ lemon
1 tsp nutritional yeast
4 tbsp agave syrup
1 tsp vanilla extract
250g Lotus biscoff biscuits
30g cacao powder

1. If you're brewing coffee, which you should be, let the coffee cool right down before carrying on.

2. Food processor. Grab it, add in the tofu, a squeeze of lemon juice, the nutritional yeast, agave syrup and vanilla. Blitz it until you've got a nicely whipped cream. Try it – it should almost taste slightly sweet but still has a nice flavour to it.

3. Now the actual bit of layering. Pour the coffee into a shallow bowl and, one-by-one, soak the biscuits in the coffee for a few seconds, then pop into a 20cm baking dish. Add two layers of biscoff biscuits and make sure there are no gaps. Add the whipped cream on top. Repeat once more until the dish is full and you're left with the whipped cream on top.

4. Using a sieve, dust the top of the cream with the cacao powder until fully coated. Crumble up one Lotus biscuit into tiny crumbs and sprinkle that over the top.

5. Now, let this set in the fridge for 2–3 hours. I am sorry. It does take time, forgive me, but don't forgive me because it's actually worth the time waiting.

6. Take it out. For a date, perhaps? No don't, just take the tiramisu out the fridge, and divvy it up with whoever you like and share it with them.

My mate Andrew's new favourite.

CALS: 441 | **PROTEIN:** 8.9g | **FAT:** 16g | **SAT FAT:** 6.2g | **CARBS:** 64g | **SUGAR:** 39g | **SALT:** 0.59g | **FIBRE:** 2g

When you think
about it . . .

... tiramisu is a
sweet lasagne

SILKY CHOCOLATE MOUSSE

Chocolate mousse is a cheat code dessert. This mousse needs literally no effort at all, but the end results are so impressive, especially knowing that this isn't a standard way to make a mousse. Also, it will impress anybody, and I mean anybody, you make it for.

*8 mins prep + 2 mins cooking + 1 hour in the fridge = **10 mins + 1 hour in the fridge total***

SERVES 2–3

170g dark chocolate
   (70% cocoa solids or above),
   broken into chunks, plus an
   extra square for the top
300g (1 block) silken tofu
1 tbsp cacao powder
2 tbsp agave syrup
pinch of salt

1. Melt the dark chocolate. You can do this one of two ways: either melt it in a microwave-safe bowl for 80 seconds at 900W, then keep stirring until the chocolate melts, or put a small saucepan on a medium heat with about 100ml of boiling water, then put a heatproof bowl on the top of that, popping the chocolate in the bowl and stirring until it melts (this is a bain-marie). You choose.

2. Next, in a food processor, blitz the melted chocolate, silken tofu, cacao powder and agave syrup until everything's combined and you have a smooth chocolatey mousse.

3. It's ready, but not technically ready. Stick it in a fancy glass or some ramekins – you should have enough for 2–3 people.

4. Chop an extra square of dark chocolate into tiny pieces, or shavings if you're feeling advanced, then top each of the mousses with that and a pinch of salt. Let it rest in the fridge for 1 hour minimum, or as long as you can. Ideally make these in the morning and enjoy them in the afternoon or evening.

5. When you're ready, enjoy the beautifully firm and chocolatey mousse you created in no time at all.

Easily the easiest dessert here.

CALS: 663 | **PROTEIN:** 16g | **FAT:** 42g | **SAT FAT:** 24g | **CARBS:** 48g | **SUGAR:** 39g | **SALT:** 0.27g | **FIBRE:** 12g

CINNAMONY CRUNCH FLAPJACKS

Jack of all, master of all, somehow.

You would think that flapjacks would be a vegan's go-to snack. But no. Most flapjacks have butter in them, and while I can see the appeal, with the price of butter costing as much as a mortgage nowadays, here's a recipe you can make that's plant-based and reminds me of that cinnamony cereal I won't name. You're gonna absolutely love it.

*10 mins prep + 17 mins cooking = **27 mins total** (bit longer, sorry)*

MAKES 12 SQUARES

baking paper (not an ingredient but something you may have to go to the shops and get)
250g porridge oats
100g pecans
6 medjool dates (without the stones)
1 ripe banana, peeled
150g coconut oil or vegan butter
1 tsp vanilla extract
2 tbsp flaxseed
3 tsp ground cinnamon
1 tbsp light brown sugar

1. Preheat oven. Please. 200°C (fan 180°C/gas mark 6). And line a baking dish (around 20cm) with baking paper.

2. Pop the oats in a large mixing bowl and let them sit. They're about to go through a meltdown in this recipe, so any time for them to prepare for that would be great.

3. Now for the food processor, oowee. Add about three-quarters of the pecans and blitz till you have little chopped pieces. Then add those into the bowl of oats. Now get the food processor back in action by adding the dates and banana and blitzing till you have a sort of paste.

4. Add the banana-date paste, the coconut oil, vanilla extract, flaxseed and 2 teaspoons of the cinnamon and mix well until everything's combined up and you've got a nice firm consistency. Not too dry but not too wet. That is very vague, but you'll understand when you feel it.

5. In a small bowl, mix the sugar and remaining teaspoon of cinnamon together. Pop the flapjack mix into the lined dish and press to the sides until you have a nice even flapjack. Now what happened to the rest of the pecans from earlier?

6. Ah they're back. Press them into the flapjack in a sort of spattered way, or uniform if you will. Then sprinkle a tiny bit of cinnamon-sugar on top and bake for 17 minutes.

7. Take it out of the oven, let it cool down completely. Meltdown over. Divvy up and devour. These will keep for up to 5 days in an airtight container.

CALS: 321 | **PROTEIN:** 4.2g | **FAT:** 21g | **SAT FAT:** 12g | **CARBS:** 26g | **SUGAR:** 12g | **SALT:** 0g | **FIBRE:** 4.1g

ELITE FRENCH TOAST

Oui oui mon amour.

That is literally the only bit of French I know. My friend Giuseppe speaks fluent French, even though he's Italian, and because he asked, I'm doing a French-ish recipe. And I think I found the perfect vegan way to recreate it. This is traditionally made with eggs and brioche, but you can't have either. Sorry. But I'm not sorry really, because this is a lovely recipe.

*6 mins prep + 12 mins cooking = **18 mins total***

SERVES 2

good dollop (40g) smooth
  almond butter
6 tbsp agave or maple syrup,
  plus a bit extra for drizzling
pinch of sea salt
150g (½ block) silken tofu
100ml plant milk (I like oat or soy)
2 tsp ground cinnamon
1 tsp cornflour
2 slices white farmhouse bread
2 tsp coconut oil or light
  olive oil
3 strawberries
2 tsp vegan yogurt
handful of pecans

1. Get a bowl out of your cupboard and dollop in the almond butter, then muddle in a tablespoon of syrup and a pinch of sea salt, mix up and put it to one side.

2. In a nice food processor, blitz up the silken tofu, milk, cinnamon, cornflour and 4 tablespoons of syrup until it's incredibly smooth. Then pour into a shallow bowl, or a plate with a lip, or a small tray. Coat a slice of bread in the mix. Essentially you want to drench the thing, but not have it fall apart, so around 10 seconds on both sides will work.

3. Now get a small frying pan, get it on a medium-high heat, and add the coconut oil or light olive oil to that pan. Once melted or hot, add your coated bread one at a time and fry for 2–3 minutes each side. It is a delicate thing, so try to be gentle when flipping it over. And if your bread starts rising up in the middle, gently press down so everything is cooking and good looking.

4. While it's frying, slice up the strawberries into little diced cubes, if you can.

5. Finish the recipe by serving one slice of toast, then spread a spoonful of the syrupy almond butter on top of that toast, then top with the other slice of toast, like a sandwich.

6. Finishing bits! Go in with a dollop of vegan yogurt, the remaining syrup and remaining almond butter, a handful of pecans, crush them if you like. And also the strawberries. Share with a mate or a date. Oui oui.

CALS: 742 | **PROTEIN:** 17g | **FAT:** 40g | **SAT FAT:** 11g | **CARBS:** 74g | **SUGAR:** 48g | **SALT:** 0.92g | **FIBRE:** 8.9g

WATERMELON SUGAR SHOTS

Someone's a Harry Styles fan.

Yes, I really am naming a dessert after a Harry Styles song and I do not care. Because these are brilliant. They aren't a dessert per se, but I would like to think they're a great kick to finish a meal, start a morning, or put with a fancy meal as a 'palette cleanser'. Enjoy. I love you, Harry.

5 mins prep + 12 mins making
= ***17 mins total***

MAKES 6 SHOTS

½ watermelon, or 2 packs of
   watermelon chunks (500–550g)
juice of 2 limes, plus another
   ½ lime to make a salt rim
15g fresh mint leaves
pinch of sea salt, plus extra for
   the salt rim
4 tbsp agave syrup
smoked paprika (optional)

TOP TIP:

To avoid waste, you can take the watermelon pulp in the sieve and pop it in an ice-cube tray with water. Then you've got some infused ice. You can also add the pulp to the Pico de Gallo con Corn recipe on page 220 and swap the corn for the pulp. Also, should you wish to make it boozy, add three shots of rum or tequila to the melon mix.

1. If you cheated and bought a pack of watermelon chunks, go to step 2. Otherwise, chop up the watermelon safely by chopping it in half on the shorter side, and then half again. Keep the other half for another recipe or just for eating leisurely. Scoop the watermelon flesh using a tablespoon and pop it into a clean bowl.

2. Put the watermelon and the remaining ingredients into a food processor and blitz until smooth. Grab a jug that can fit in your fridge and put a sieve on top of it. Take a breath before this next step.

3. Pour the watermelon mix through the sieve into the jug and continue until all the liquid has passed through. Use a spoon to stir and squeeze the liquid out until you're left with the pulp (don't worry, I have a use for this). Leave it in the fridge to chill out a bit, while you also chill out a bit, because you deserve to – chopping a melon is hard. Unless you didn't chop the melon, in which case, flick back in the book and make another recipe of mine.

4. Finish the recipe by being extra. Rub the half lime on the rim of your shot glasses. Add two pinches of salt into a small bowl and stir in a pinch of paprika, if you like. Rub the shot glasses rim-down in the salt. Stand up the glasses and pour the watermelon mix into them. This will serve up a lot of shots. You can also mix 100ml of the watermelon mix with about 200ml of good lemonade for a watermelon lemonade.

5. Serve to your mates, and feel refreshed, genuinely.

CALS: 76 | **PROTEIN:** 0.5g | **FAT:** 0.5g | **SAT FAT:** 0g | **CARBS:** 17g | **SUGAR:** 16g | **SALT:** 0.56g | **FIBRE:** 0g

SNACKS

5

THE DEFINITION OF YOU, MATE

Snacks make the world go round, that's a quote somewhere by someone.

Everyone loves a snack. And these are the snacks that will fulfil any cravings. You'll not even think of grabbing a chocolate bar or some roasted nuts.

I basically sat there and thought 'what would be a snack that you'd go back for?' and most of the time, it's all of these lot. There's a good few smoothie recipes in here, some protein balls that taste like a cake, and a spinach satay you'll try to serve with everything you make.

HOLY HARISSA HUMMUS

Dip of the gods.

I love hummus, vegans love hummus, people love hummus, we all love hummus. There are many recipes out there that make the god-crafted dip, and I am well aware that mine is not the perfect recipe, but it's a great foolproof one to get people starting to make their own hummus. As well as being a delicious dip, it also works brilliantly with some of the dishes in this book, so go back on yourself, and see where this hummus works best. It's probably the kebab on page 140 to be honest.

2 mins prep + 5 mins making = 7 mins total

SERVES 4 AS A SNACK

1 x 400g tin chickpeas
1 garlic clove
1 tsp ground cumin
4 tbsp tahini
2 tbsp rose harissa (it is optional but it is in the recipe title, so please do it)
1 lemon, plus 1 for good luck
2 tbsp extra virgin olive oil, plus more for good luck
good pinch of sea salt
100ml ice-cold water

1. Drain the chickpeas in a colander and rinse quickly with cold running water. Add them to a food processor along with the garlic, cumin, tahini, harissa and the juice from 1 lemon. Add the olive oil and salt, then blitz. This will form a thick paste that will resemble a very thick hummus.

2. Now gradually add the water to the mix. This will help lighten up the hummus and make it luxuriously smooth. At this point, the cook in you will kick in. You will need to add salt, more lemon juice, olive oil and harissa paste (if using) to your taste. What you're after is that classic hummus taste with a freshness and also the kick from the harissa still coming through (again, if you're using it). Add as much of these three to your liking and blitz until smooth. Oh, and it's also beautifully orange.

3. Once you've got that, dip in, with bread, pitta or whatever you'd like, you do you, boo.

TOP TIP:

For an even smoother hummus, you can remove the skins from the chickpeas, but in all honesty, it takes a lot longer, and as much as I like it, I don't do it often. Up to you though.

CALS: 321 | **PROTEIN:** 8.6g | **FAT:** 26g | **SAT FAT:** 3.6g | **CARBS:** 11g | **SUGAR:** 0.8g | **SALT:** 0.55g | **FIBRE:** 5.1g

TEMPEH NUGGETS

As good as the chicken ones.

Tempeh is fermented soy beans, pressed into a block. Because of that, it has an acquired taste, and a bitter aftertaste that, I can't lie, can put new people off. So the question came to me: how the hell do I make people love tempeh as much as chicken, or at least slightly more than before? Make them into nuggets. That was my favourite and best solution after months of rigorous testing and eating. If you love nuggets, then you're in luck, because these are essentially them. Brilliant little things.

*7 mins prep + 11 mins cooking = **18 mins total***

SERVES 2

800ml boiling water
2 veg stock cubes
200g (1 block) tempeh
50g cornflour
80ml oat milk
50g panko breadcrumbs
2 tsp ground cumin
2 tsp smoked paprika
salt and pepper

TOP TIP:

Use one hand to batter the tempeh in the cornflour and milk, then the other hand for the breadcrumbs only. Keep that hand clean then you end up with nuggets with nice even distribution of breadcrumbs rather than clumps. And also, you can oven-bake these for 20 minutes with a bit of oil on top - 200°C (fan 180°C/gas mark 6) - or, dare I say it, air-fry these boys in 10 minutes.

1. First up; stock. Pop the boiling water and stock cubes in a small saucepan, mix well and let it bubble away on a medium heat.

2. Now this tempeh, let's sort it out. Chop up the block to make nuggets – ideally I like them bite-size and not too chunky. Then pop those into the stock for 5 minutes. This is going to help get rid of the bitter taste of tempeh.

3. While you're waiting, make a breading station with three bowls: cornflour in one bowl, oat milk in another bowl, and breadcrumbs in the final bowl. Add a teaspoon of each of the spices to the cornflour, and another teaspoon of them into the breadcrumbs. Season the cornflour and breadcrumbs with salt and pepper too, then mix them both well, still in their separate bowls btw.

4. When the tempeh is in stock (another joke for you there), pop a sieve on top of a heatproof jug or another saucepan and pour the tempeh out. You can use that stock for another recipe.

5. Batter the tempeh by coating it in cornflour, then milk, then breadcrumbs, then fry in a pan with olive oil on a medium-high heat for 1–2 minutes on each side until the nuggets are crispy and golden like Harry Styles. I don't know if he's crispy. Might be, who knows?

6. Get a plate ready for the nuggets, lined with kitchen paper, and pop the nuggets there once cooked, to drain off any excess oil.

7. Serve on a jazzy plate, with all the dips. Ketchup, BBQ sauce, mayo, whatever you can get your hands on.

CALS: 504 | **PROTEIN:** 25g | **FAT:** 24g | **SAT FAT:** 2.5g | **CARBS:** 42g | **SUGAR:** 2.9g | **SALT:** 4.7g | **FIBRE:** 11g

SPINACH SATAY SIDE

That's a lot of 'S's.

Spinach is a powerful ingredient. Not only does it pack in loads of iron, but it also has loads of vitamins and a little boost of protein in it, making it a brilliant ingredient. The problem? It's proper boring. So, let me give you one of many ways you can make this spinach into a side dish that would make Popeye go 'ayy, that's banging pal'.

*5 mins prep + 8 mins cooking = **13 mins total***

SERVES 2 AS A SIDE DISH

2 spring onions (white parts only)
2cm (¾in) piece of ginger
light olive oil, for frying
200g baby spinach
1 tsp white miso paste
1 tbsp smooth peanut butter
1 tsp agave syrup
25ml hot water
1 tbsp sesame oil
2 tbsp mirin
1 tsp white sesame seeds
½ lime
salt and pepper

1. Slice up the spring onions into thin slices and grate the ginger so it's nice and fine, then fry with a little oil in a large frying pan on a medium heat. Season with salt and pepper and after 3–4 minutes, or when they are both golden and starting to crisp, add all the spinach.

2. While the spinach is wilting, it's satay time. Well, it's more of a peanut miso dressing but brilliant nevertheless. In a small jug, mix the miso paste, peanut butter, agave syrup, hot water, sesame oil and mirin together until it forms a lovely sauce.

3. Once the spinach has wilted, turn the heat down to low and pour the sauce all over it, mixing well and making sure everything is covered.

4. Once the spinach is cooked and the sauce has reduced, serve sprinkled with the sesame seeds, a squeeze of lime juice, on the side of anything Asian-inspired in this book.

CALS: 260 | **PROTEIN:** 6.1g | **FAT:** 19g | **SAT FAT:** 3.3g | **CARBS:** 11g | **SUGAR:** 9.2g | **SALT:** 0.66g | **FIBRE:** 2.2g

SWEET & SALTY TORTILLA CHIPS

Stop it, but on a real, make these.

This brilliant snack might already be on your radar. Tortilla chips, we love them, we need them, in everything. However, are there any sweet tortilla chips? I personally thought that, and so did my mate Steph Elswood. So this is essentially me giving her the recipe, in a mass-printed format. Also, don't write this off: it is, without a doubt, an absolute winner.

*6 mins prep + 6 mins cooking = **12 mins total***

SERVES 4

6 tortilla wraps
1 tsp ground cinnamon
pinch of sea salt
2 tbsp light brown sugar
peanut butter or almond butter,
  to serve (optional)

1. Oven. On. 180°C (fan 160°C/gas mark 4). Please. Thanks hun.

2. Lay all the tortillas on top of each other, then chop in half, then half again, then half again, then half again, until you end up with a load of little triangles, shaped like tortilla chips. Mental, isn't it?

3. Lay all those tortillas in a single layer on a large baking tray. In a small bowl, mix the cinnamon, salt and sugar together, then sprinkle evenly over the top of all the tortillas. Bake for 6 minutes in the oven until properly crispy.

4. Serve with peanut butter, almond butter, or just snack on it like popcorn. Why not? You can even crumble them up and use them as a topping on desserts, or just a plain old bowl of oats.

CALS: 356 | **PROTEIN:** 10g | **FAT:** 9.8g | **SAT FAT:** 3.4g | **CARBS:** 55g | **SUGAR:** 12g | **SALT:** 1.6g | **FIBRE:** 4.1g

BEAUT BERRY GRANOLA POTS

Pots of gold. If the gold was berry coloured.

Yogurt pots are brilliant. If you remember back in the day when there would be this advert of a girl winning marbles from this bloke who took them from another boy, you'll remember she won them because she ate a yogurt pot. I don't know if I'm allowed to say the name of the yogurt company due to copyright but you get the point. Now we're doing it plant-based, in your face, let's go.

*10 mins prep + 5 mins cooking = **15 mins total***

SERVES 2

150g mixed berries (raspberries, strawberries, blueberries, blackberries, whatever's in season)
2 tbsp agave syrup
2 empty, clean jam jars – make sure you have them!
200g vegan Greek-style yogurt

For the granola crumble
50g porridge oats
2 tbsp desiccated coconut
100g unsalted mixed nuts
1 tbsp flaxseed
1 tsp ground cinnamon
2 medjool dates (without the stones)
black pepper, bonkers? Yes.

TOP TIP:

This makes more granola than you need for this recipe. Save the rest for more pots or enjoy on top of porridge, as a crumble topping … the choices are endless!

1. Pop the oats, coconut, nuts, flaxseed, cinnamon and dates in a food processor and blitz until you essentially have a crumble. Add the tiniest crack of black pepper.

2. Toast the mixture in a large frying pan on a medium heat for 2–3 minutes, with no oil in the pan. Turn the heat off once that's done.

3. Next up, get all the berries and blitz them in a food processor (or chop them roughly), then add those to a small saucepan on a medium heat. Squeeze in the agave syrup and let it bubble away until the berries are reduced and looking almost jammy. Turn off the heat and let it cool.

4. Once both the granola and the berry jam are cool, layer up your jam jars. Go with a bit of jam on the bottom, then loads of yogurt, another tablespoon of jam and finally 2 tablespoons of granola per pot. Now do me a favour, please? Enjoy it. It's perfect for when you're on the go, with whatever you've got going on in your lives.

CALS: 305 | **PROTEIN:** 11g | **FAT:** 13g | **SAT FAT:** 2.9g | **CARBS:** 34g | **SUGAR:** 26g | **SALT:** 0.37g | **FIBRE:** 6.2g

FROZEN PEANUT BUTTER & BANANA BITES

Funny to see an English person making a frozen snack isn't it? You're probably reading this and it's not even sunny outside. I wrote and made this recipe when there was a huge old heatwave in 2022, and genuinely when I say this helped, it helped. It's creamy, refreshing and essentially like a little chocolate ice cream in your hand. Well, if it is sunny, and you're reading this, then brilliant, this one is perfect for you.

*10 mins prep + 1–2 hours in the freezer = **longer than 20 minutes in total to make it** (forgive me)*

MAKES ABOUT 20 BITES

2 medium bananas (size matters)

4 tbsp good-quality crunchy peanut butter

1 tbsp vegan vanilla protein powder (optional)

180g dark chocolate (70% cocoa solids or above)

1 tsp coconut oil

1. Peel and chop the bananas into 2cm chunks, then put them in a bowl. In another small bowl, mix the peanut butter and the protein powder (if using), together, forever.

2. Make sure you've got space in your freezer btw. Get a thin rectangular tray and line it with baking paper, then pop the banana chunks on the tray face up. Spoon a teaspoon-sized dollop of peanut butter on top of each banana chunk so it covers it nicely.

3. Break up the chocolate into a bowl and either melt in a microwave for 1 minute or melt over a bain marie (we spoke about this in the Silky Chocolate Mousse recipe on page 178). Once the chocolate is melted, stir in the teaspoon of coconut oil. Finally, pour 2 teaspoons of melted chocolate over each banana chunk one at a time. Then pop the coated banana back onto the baking tray.

4. Once you've done that, get it in the freezer for 1–2 hours. I can't lie, this is the most fiddly of my desserts, but trust me, like those hair adverts used to say, you're worth it.

5. After freezing, break them off the tray and devour on a hot day. These will keep in an airtight container in the freezer for up to 1 month.

Personal best with peanut butter.

CALS: 93 | **PROTEIN:** 2.6g | **FAT:** 6.5g | **SAT FAT:** 3.1g | **CARBS:** 5.3g | **SUGAR:** 4.4g | **SALT:** 0.08g | **FIBRE:** 1.6g

CARROT CAKE PROTEIN BALLS

A classic cake in a circular shape.

My brother Max's favourite cake is a carrot cake. And in this day and age, where it's not socially acceptable or all that healthy to eat a carrot cake every day, I thought I'd make something that brings you that flavour in a quick, satisfying format. Quite like my recipe videos, how charming.

*2 mins prep + 8 mins making = **10 mins total***

MAKES 8—10 BALLS

1 medium carrot
10 medjool dates (without the stones)
50g pecans
50g walnuts
30g (handful of) sultanas
1 scoop (30g) vegan vanilla protein powder
2 tsp ground cinnamon
1 tsp ground allspice
pinch of sea salt
40g desiccated coconut

1. Grate the carrot using a box grater then leave it alone. It's just been grated, give it some time to think.

2. Blitz the dates, pecans and walnuts in a food processor until combined and smooth, but sticky. Add all the other ingredients except for the desiccated coconut to the food processor and stir until fully combined in a big old mix. You wanna stir as the texture's better. If you blitz again you end up with one big, gloopy mess.

3. Tip the desiccated coconut into a large shallow bowl and then, with damp hands (sounds very cheffy, but it just means slightly wet your hands), shape part of the mix into a ball, then coat it in coconut – make the balls however big you'd like, by the way. Do this for the rest of the mixture until you've got nothing left.

4. You can eat them now if you'd like or eat them whenever. These will keep for up to a week in an airtight container in the fridge.

CALS: 249 | **PROTEIN:** 4.7g | **FAT:** 12g | **SAT FAT:** 3.6g | **CARBS:** 27g | **SUGAR:** 24g | **SALT:** 0.22g | **FIBRE:** 5.4g

BLUEBERRY BANOFFEE SMOOTHIE

Set the scene: you fancy a smoothie, combine a load of ingredients together, blitz it and hope for the best. Well, that's what I did, and I ended up with this incredible smoothie that was not only fruity, but tasted just like banoffee pie. I don't know how, but here we are. By the way, this is one of the first smoothie recipes I made when I became a vegan. 'Oh wow', you're probably saying sarcastically.

5 mins prep + 1 min making
*= **6 mins total***

SERVES 2

100g frozen blueberries
½ banana
1 scoop (30g) vegan vanilla
  protein powder
250ml plant milk (oat or soy
  milk works best)
1 tbsp agave syrup
1 tbsp hemp seeds (optional)

1. Blitz all the ingredients up in a blender until cool, combined, and a smooth operator.

2. There's not a second step, apart from drinking the smoothie. Bye.

Somehow tastes of banoffee and that's good for you.

CALS: 209 | **PROTEIN:** 14g | **FAT:** 7.4g | **SAT FAT:** 0.9g | **CARBS:** 19g | **SUGAR:** 12g | **SALT:** 0.61g | **FIBRE:** 5.6g

ULTIMATE CHOCOLATE SMOOTHIE

Say less.

I love chocolate. I think it's pretty evident considering half the desserts in here have chocolate in them. So, if ever, like me, you fancy more chocolate in your life, then make this smoothie. Because why not?

*5 mins prep = **5 mins total***

SERVES 2

200ml plant milk (I like oat
  or soya)
1 tbsp cacao powder
1 tsp red miso paste
1 square of dark chocolate
60g (handful of) ice cubes
1 scoop (30g) vegan vanilla
  protein powder
1 tsp agave syrup

1. We'll do this in one step. Blitz all the ingredients in a blender until smooth and quite thick. If too thin, add more ice, if too thick, add more milk. Drink it. You're welcome.

Pictured with the Blueberry Banoffee Smoothie on page 205

CALS: 138 | **PROTEIN:** 12g | **FAT:** 6g | **SAT FAT:** 1.6g | **CARBS:** 6.5g | **SUGAR:** 3.5g | **SALT:** 0.86g | **FIBRE:** 4.4g

GET-YOUR-GREENS -IN SMOOTHIE

Just what the doctor would order.

I'm not actually entirely sure what my or your doctor would order. But for me, if there's a way of sneaking green veg into things and making it taste unexpectedly great, I'll find it. Such as this green smoothie. It's a great way of boosting your iron intake, a mineral so many people bang on about vegans not getting enough of. It's creamy, it's dreamy, and you'll love it.

*5 mins prep = **5 mins total***

SERVES 2

1 ripe banana
250ml plant milk (I like oat or
  soya)
50g (handful of) spinach
1 tsp hemp seeds
60g (handful of) ice cubes
1 tsp peanut butter
1 scoop (30g) vegan vanilla
  protein powder
1 tsp agave syrup

1. Chop the banana up into small chunks then blitz all the ingredients in a blender until smooth and quite thick. Again, if it's too thin, add more ice, if too thick, add more milk.

2. Et voilà. Give it to your doctor, or if you're a doctor reading this, enjoy it yourself, with an apple.

 Pictured with the Blueberry Banoffee Smoothie on page 205

CALS: 213 | **PROTEIN:** 15g | **FAT:** 8.7g | **SAT FAT:** 1.6g | **CARBS:** 16g | **SUGAR:** 13g | **SALT:** 0.75g | **FIBRE:** 5.5g

PICK-
ME-UPS

6

THE BOOST YOUR MEAL DESERVES

Pick me up when your food is feeling down.

I call these 'pick-me-ups' because they take your already brilliant meal and elevate it to a 12/10. They also pair well with a lot of the recipes in this book, so enjoy.

There's a brilliant topping for pastas, my favourite salsas including one that my Auntie Carmel demanded for me to put in this book, and if I didn't she'd disown me, and sauces that pair well with the kebab and curry recipes in this book. So do me a favour, if you need it, if you're cooking a recipe that's not in this book, liven up your meals with these lot!

THE PARMIGIANO ALTERNATIVO

I'm sorry Italy.

You know Parmesan, otherwise known as the one that got away for vegans. Well, here's your alternative that you can sprinkle on anything you used to use Parmesan for. It's not only just like Parmesan, but it sure as hell looks like it too, and it's a great little number to use when you'd like. Keep it in a jar or an old empty spice bottle and it should keep for a good few months.

*2 mins prep = **2 mins total***

MAKES ABOUT 5 TBSP

3 tbsp ground almonds
2 tbsp nutritional yeast
pinch of sea salt
1 tsp garlic powder (optional)

Pick-Me-Ups

1. Put all the ingredients into a small bowl and mix them together. Press down firmly on the mix to break up the nutritional yeast into smaller bits.

2. That is genuinely it. Sprinkle it on your pasta, top your salads, or your sandwiches if you'd like. Here, I've served it with the Cherry Tomato Rigatoni (see page 125). Boom.

CALS: 94 | **PROTEIN:** 5.4g | **FAT:** 6.9g | **SAT FAT:** 0.6g | **CARBS:** 1.7g | **SUGAR:** 1.1g | **SALT:** 0.11g | **FIBRE:** 2.6g

TAHINI SAUCE

A simple yet delicious way of making the sauce that might as well go on everything. It works as a dip for your sides, a drizzle for your salads, but more importantly, it makes a great sauce for your kebabs. Which, I must admit, is essential for me.

2 mins prep + 3 mins making
*= **5 mins total***

MAKES ABOUT 150ML

1 garlic clove
1 lemon
4 tbsp tahini
1 tsp white miso paste
1 tbsp extra virgin olive oil
pinch of sea salt
50ml warm water
salt and pepper

1. Grate or finely chop the garlic clove. Also, once that's done, chop the lemon in half. That's all the prep. Easy like a Sunday morning.

2. In a small bowl, mix the tahini, the lemon juice from one lemon half, the garlic, miso paste, olive oil and salt together and gradually add the warm water. You might not need all the water, but keep mixing together until you have a smooth and saucy sauce. Yes, I've used the word 'saucy' to describe the sauce.

3. And that's it. Season to taste with salt and pepper and drizzle on anything you desire. As long as it's edible, of course. I like it with my Tofu Shish Kebabs (see page 98). Store it in the fridge and, when you want to use it, add a splash of warm water to bring it back to life again. It should keep for a week, if you don't eat it all by then.

CALS: 148 | **PROTEIN:** 4.2g | **FAT:** 14g | **SAT FAT:** 2g | **CARBS:** 0.7g | **SUGAR:** 0.5g | **SALT:** 0.38g | **FIBRE:** 1.5g

JALAPEÑO & GRAPE SALSA

Kicking, fruity, and a game changer.

A salsa is a fundamental for any dinner party, even if the dinner party is a Sunday roast. Reason being? The dips. Nine times out of ten, when you go to a dinner party someone's got the dips out, along with some supermarket own-brand crisps and - hopefully, as they're my favourite - salted tortilla chips. This salsa is essentially the new kid on the block; it's the fruity and spicy number every mum wants the recipe for, and every dad wants to take home to show how much heat they can handle. An absolute winner.

*5 mins prep + 5 mins cooking = **10 mins total***

MAKES ABOUT 500ML

1 green pepper
1 jalapeño pepper
170g green seedless grapes
15g fresh mint leaves
15g fresh coriander
juice of 1 lime, plus extra if needed
salt

1. Chop the green pepper into quarters and deseed both the jalapeño and the green peppers. Char up the peppers using a non-stick large frying pan on the highest heat or directly on the hob for around 5 minutes. At this point, wash your hands, and thank me later for no chilli in your eyes.

2. Once charred, blitz everything in a food processor until smooth and chunky. Season to taste with salt and more lime juice if you need to.

3. Also, let that have a sit down in the fridge to let the flavours mingle and cool down.

4. Serve with some tortilla chips, or your chilli, or even a platter of tacos.

TOP TIP:

If you have a griddle pan handy, you can cook the peppers on there instead.

CALS: 18 | **PROTEIN:** 0.5g | **FAT:** 0g | **SAT FAT:** 0g | **CARBS:** 3.4g | **SUGAR:** 3.2g | **SALT:** 0.07g | **FIBRE:** 0.6g

RAITA, MY WAY

It has a secret ingredient.

A raita is a brilliant and fresh yogurty side that is great for pimping up your curries and for dipping your naans in. Mine isn't only vegan but Steve Jobs' favourite fruit makes an appearance too; the apple.

*10 mins prep = **10 mins total***

MAKES ABOUT 400ML

½ cucumber
½ apple
15g fresh mint leaves
juice of 1 lime
1 garlic clove
200g vegan Greek-style yogurt
  (I use the Oatly brand)
salt

1. Leaving the skin on, grate the cucumber and apple onto a clean tea towel, then wrap up the towel and squeeze as much water out as you can. Pop it into a food processor once complete.

2. Pop the mint leaves into that food processor with the cucumber–apple mix. Peel the garlic clove and add that in, then go in with the vegan yogurt, lime juice and a pinch of salt and blitz all the ingredients until smooth.

3. Transfer to the fridge to chill out for a bit and serve when you're ready, mate.

TOP TIP:

I prefer to use a food processor, but if you like you can also do it by hand the old-fashioned way.

CALS: 62 | **PROTEIN:** 4g | **FAT:** 2.2g | **SAT FAT:** 0.3g | **CARBS:** 5.4g | **SUGAR:** 4.7g | **SALT:** 0.31g | **FIBRE:** 1.5g

PICO DE GALLO CON CORN

Pico de gallo is a fresh and kicking salsa that you can serve with tacos, chillies or on top of anything really. And, not to be corny (ahaha), but the charred sweetcorn makes for a great new tweak to the classic (it's an idea that my sister came up with, by the way). This one's an essential of mine and will keep in the fridge for a good few days.

*10 mins prep + 6 mins cooking = **16 mins total***

SERVES 4 AS A SIDE

2 beef tomatoes
½ red onion
juice of 1 lime
light olive oil, for frying
70g frozen sweetcorn (or ½ small tin of sweetcorn)
15g fresh coriander
salt

1. Chop the tomato into quarters then scoop out the watery part with a spoon (basically the seeds) and discard.

2. Dice up the tomato flesh and the onion too, then mix all together with the lime juice and a pinch of salt. Leave to pickle up in the fridge for however long you want.

3. Grab a frying pan and add a tiny bit of oil to the pan. Heat up the pan on a medium-high heat and chuck in the sweetcorn. You then want to essentially char, or burn, the corn. Pop a lid on the frying pan to stop the kernels of corn from flying in your face and saying 'you wanna deal with me?'. Fry the corn for about 3 minutes on each side to get this effect. Once charred, take the pan off the heat and leave to cool down for a minute or two.

4. While that corny action is happening, chop up the coriander and mix in with the tomatoes and onions. Add the charred corn and that, once mixed, is your salsa done. That's about it. Season to taste and serve it with some lovely tortilla chips like I've got in the photo because I got hungry during the photos being taken.

A classic, but done by me.

CALS: 88 | **PROTEIN:** 1.6g | **FAT:** 3.6g | **SAT FAT:** 0.5g | **CARBS:** 9.7g | **SUGAR:** 6.3g | **SALT:** 0.14g | **FIBRE:** 2.1g

THE PLAN FOR PEOPLE ON THEIR OWN

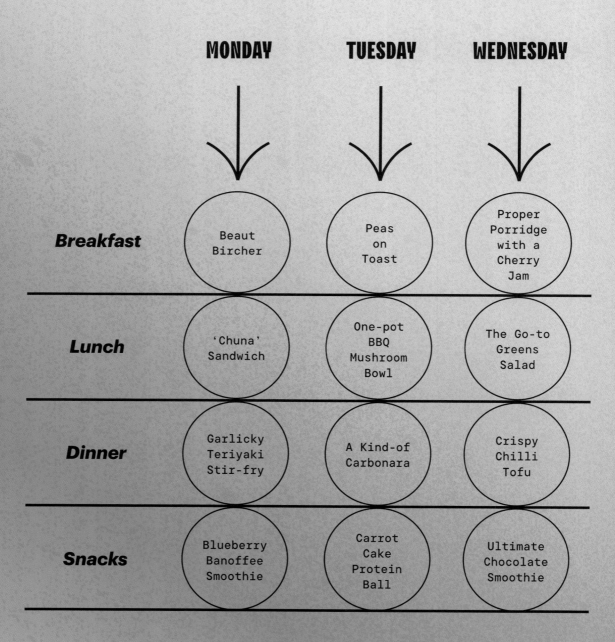

	MONDAY	**TUESDAY**	**WEDNESDAY**
Breakfast	Beaut Bircher	Peas on Toast	Proper Porridge with a Cherry Jam
Lunch	'Chuna' Sandwich	One-pot BBQ Mushroom Bowl	The Go-to Greens Salad
Dinner	Garlicky Teriyaki Stir-fry	A Kind-of Carbonara	Crispy Chilli Tofu
Snacks	Blueberry Banoffee Smoothie	Carrot Cake Protein Ball	Ultimate Chocolate Smoothie

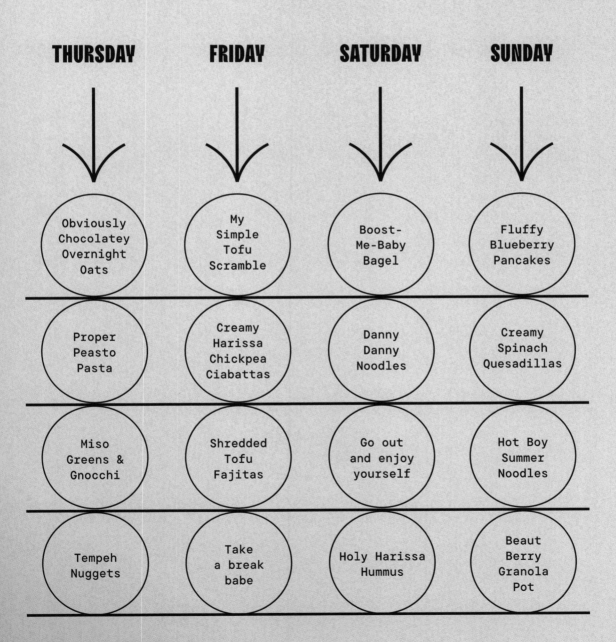

THURSDAY	FRIDAY	SATURDAY	SUNDAY
Obviously Chocolatey Overnight Oats	My Simple Tofu Scramble	Boost-Me-Baby Bagel	Fluffy Blueberry Pancakes
Proper Peasto Pasta	Creamy Harissa Chickpea Ciabattas	Danny Danny Noodles	Creamy Spinach Quesadillas
Miso Greens & Gnocchi	Shredded Tofu Fajitas	Go out and enjoy yourself	Hot Boy Summer Noodles
Tempeh Nuggets	Take a break babe	Holy Harissa Hummus	Beaut Berry Granola Pot

THE PLAN FOR LOVED-UP PEOPLE (COUPLES)

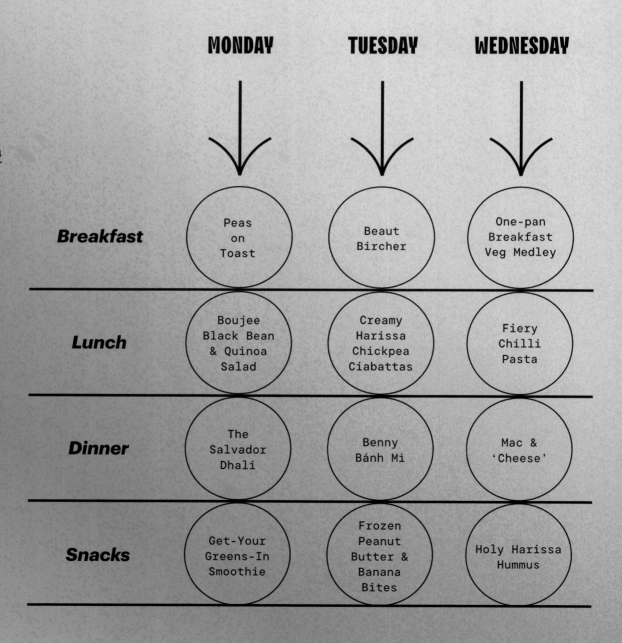

	MONDAY	**TUESDAY**	**WEDNESDAY**
Breakfast	Peas on Toast	Beaut Bircher	One-pan Breakfast Veg Medley
Lunch	Boujee Black Bean & Quinoa Salad	Creamy Harissa Chickpea Ciabattas	Fiery Chilli Pasta
Dinner	The Salvador Dhali	Benny Bánh Mì	Mac & 'Cheese'
Snacks	Get-Your Greens-In Smoothie	Frozen Peanut Butter & Banana Bites	Holy Harissa Hummus

THURSDAY   FRIDAY   SATURDAY   SUNDAY

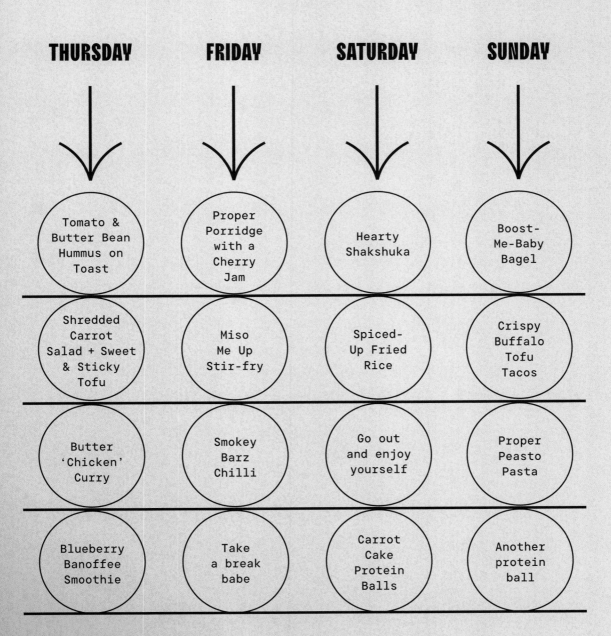

THURSDAY	FRIDAY	SATURDAY	SUNDAY
Tomato & Butter Bean Hummus on Toast	Proper Porridge with a Cherry Jam	Hearty Shakshuka	Boost-Me-Baby Bagel
Shredded Carrot Salad + Sweet & Sticky Tofu	Miso Me Up Stir-fry	Spiced-Up Fried Rice	Crispy Buffalo Tofu Tacos
Butter 'Chicken' Curry	Smokey Barz Chilli	Go out and enjoy yourself	Proper Peasto Pasta
Blueberry Banoffee Smoothie	Take a break babe	Carrot Cake Protein Balls	Another protein ball

THE PLAN FOR YOU AND THE PARTNER AND THE KIDS (FAMILIES)

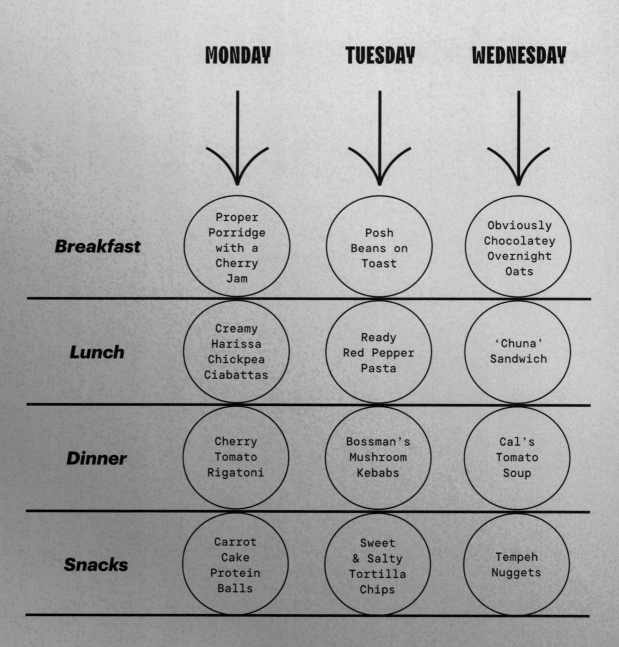

	MONDAY	**TUESDAY**	**WEDNESDAY**
Breakfast	Proper Porridge with a Cherry Jam	Posh Beans on Toast	Obviously Chocolatey Overnight Oats
Lunch	Creamy Harissa Chickpea Ciabattas	Ready Red Pepper Pasta	'Chuna' Sandwich
Dinner	Cherry Tomato Rigatoni	Bossman's Mushroom Kebabs	Cal's Tomato Soup
Snacks	Carrot Cake Protein Balls	Sweet & Salty Tortilla Chips	Tempeh Nuggets

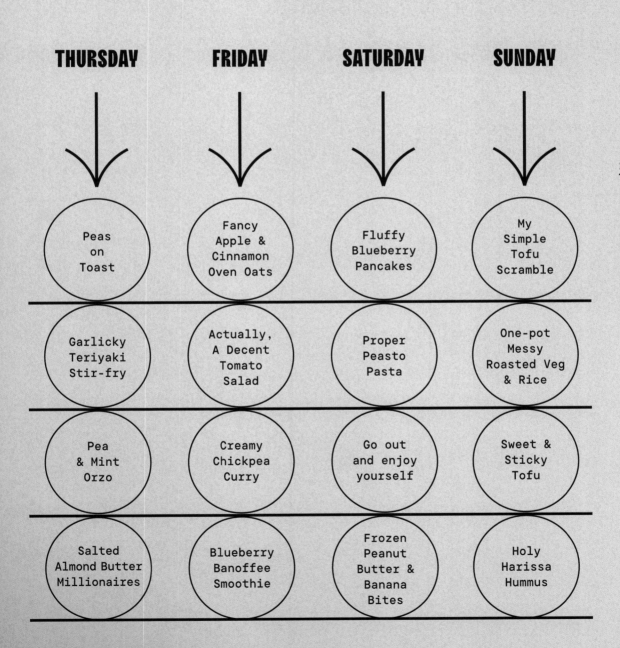

THURSDAY

- Peas on Toast
- Garlicky Teriyaki Stir-fry
- Pea & Mint Orzo
- Salted Almond Butter Millionaires

FRIDAY

- Fancy Apple & Cinnamon Oven Oats
- Actually, A Decent Tomato Salad
- Creamy Chickpea Curry
- Blueberry Banoffee Smoothie

SATURDAY

- Fluffy Blueberry Pancakes
- Proper Peasto Pasta
- Go out and enjoy yourself
- Frozen Peanut Butter & Banana Bites

SUNDAY

- My Simple Tofu Scramble
- One-pot Messy Roasted Veg & Rice
- Sweet & Sticky Tofu
- Holy Harissa Hummus

THE PLAN FOR THE FIRST-TIME COOKS

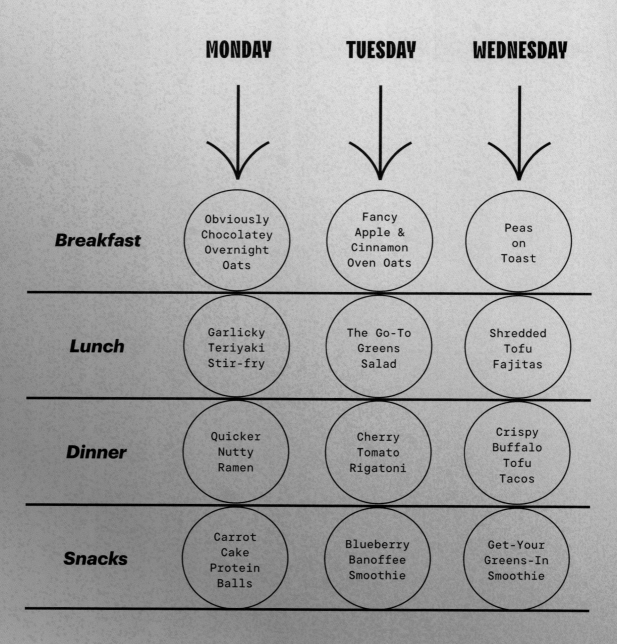

	MONDAY	**TUESDAY**	**WEDNESDAY**
Breakfast	Obviously Chocolatey Overnight Oats	Fancy Apple & Cinnamon Oven Oats	Peas on Toast
Lunch	Garlicky Teriyaki Stir-fry	The Go-To Greens Salad	Shredded Tofu Fajitas
Dinner	Quicker Nutty Ramen	Cherry Tomato Rigatoni	Crispy Buffalo Tofu Tacos
Snacks	Carrot Cake Protein Balls	Blueberry Banoffee Smoothie	Get-Your Greens-In Smoothie

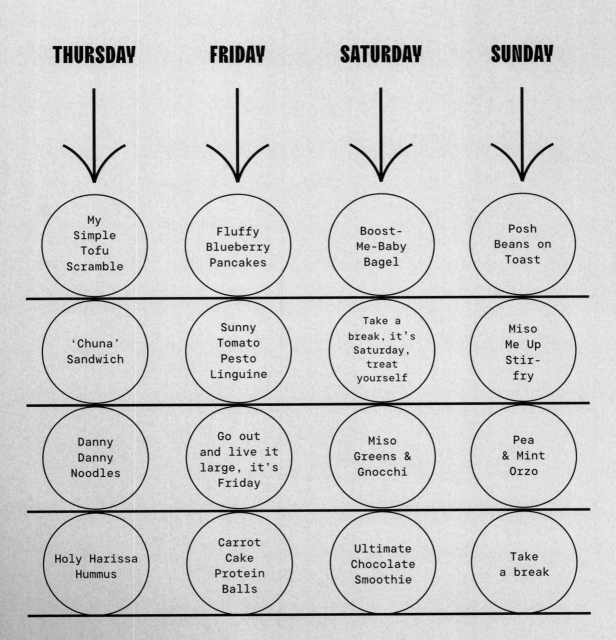

THURSDAY	FRIDAY	SATURDAY	SUNDAY
My Simple Tofu Scramble	Fluffy Blueberry Pancakes	Boost-Me-Baby Bagel	Posh Beans on Toast
'Chuna' Sandwich	Sunny Tomato Pesto Linguine	Take a break, it's Saturday, treat yourself	Miso Me Up Stir-fry
Danny Danny Noodles	Go out and live it large, it's Friday	Miso Greens & Gnocchi	Pea & Mint Orzo
Holy Harissa Hummus	Carrot Cake Protein Balls	Ultimate Chocolate Smoothie	Take a break

INDEX

Note: **page numbers in bold refer to illustrations.**

A

agave syrup 15
almond (ground)
    creamy chickpea curry 112
    the parmigiano alternativo 212
almond butter 12
    elite French toast 183
    salted almond butter millionaires 168, **169–71**
    soft-baked choc & coffee cookies 166
    Thai-style peanut butter curry 93
apple
    beaut bircher 38
    fancy apple & cinnamon oven oats 34, **35**
    raita, my way 218
apple cider vinegar 15
avocado 128

B

bagel, boost-me-baby 44, **45**
balsamic vinegar 12
banana
    blueberry banoffee smoothie 204, **205**
    cinnamon crunch flapjacks 180
    fancy apple & cinnamon oven oats 34
    fluffy blueberry pancakes 30
    frozen peanut butter & banana bites 200, **201**
    get-your-greens-in smoothie 207
    miso banana crumble 162, **163**
    one-pan cookie 164
bánh mì, Benny 118, **119**
basil
    the go-to greens salad 68
    Green Goddess soup 90
    one-pot messy veg & rice 102
    proper peasto pasta 104
    ready red pepper pasta 78
    sunny tomato pesto linguine 88
batch cooking 23
bean(s)
    boujee black bean & quinoa salad 64, 65
    jackfruit chipotle burritos 128
    one-pan breakfast veg medley 51
    one-pot BBQ mushroom rice bowl 60
    posh beans on toast 46, **47**
    smoky barz chilli 126
    tomato & butter bean hummus on toast 42, 43
    see also edamame bean
beansprouts 76
berries
    beaut berry granola pots 198, **199**
    elite French toast 183
    obviously chocolatey overnight oats 37
    see also blueberry
bircher, beaut 38

black bean
    boujee black bean & quinoa salad **64**, 65
    jackfruit chipotle burritos 128
    one-pot BBQ mushroom rice bowl 60
    smoky barz chilli 126
blueberry
    blueberry banoffee smoothie 204, **205**
    blueberry jam 30, **31–3**
    fluffy blueberry pancakes 30, **31–3**
bread
    Green Goddess soup 90
    see also toast
breadcrumbs
    fiery chilli pasta 100
    mac & 'cheese' 137
    proper peasto pasta 104
    see also panko breadcrumbs
broccoli see Tenderstem broccoli
brunch 25–53
budgets 11
burger sauce 130–2
burgers, tempeh smash 130–3, **131–2**
burritos, jackfruit chipotle 128, **129**
butter bean
    posh beans on toast 46, **47**
    tomato & butter bean hummus on toast 42, **43**
butter 'chicken' (well actually tofu) curry 120–3,
    121–2

C

cabbage (red), crispy buffalo tofu tacos 156, **157**
cacao nib(s) 28, 37
cacao powder
    Mosconi's tiramisu 174
    obviously chocolatey overnight oats 37
    silky chocolate mousse 178
    soft-baked choc & coffee cookies 166
    ultimate chocolate smoothie 206
cannellini bean
    beans on toast 46, **47**
    one-pan breakfast veg medley 51
caper brine 73
carbonara, a kind-of 114, 115–17
carrot
    carrot cake protein balls **202**, 203
    garlicky teriyaki stir-fry 94
    pickled carrot 118
    shredded carrot salad 66, **67**
    simply, a noodle soup 81
    the ultimate quick Bolognese 134

cashew nut
    creamy spinach quesadillas 84, **85**
    a kind-of carbonara 114

mac & 'cheese' 137
proper peasto pasta 104
sunny tomato pesto linguine 88, **89**
Thai-style peanut butter curry 93
cavolo nero 81
cherry jam 28
chickpea(s)
    actually, a decent tomato salad 74
    'chuna' sandwich 73
    creamy chickpea curry 112, **113**
    creamy harissa chickpea ciabattas 58, **59**
    the go-to greens salad 68
    holy harissa hummus 190
    smoky barz chilli 126
    Thai-style peanut butter curry 93
    tomatoey chickpea & broccoli curry 146, **147**
chilli (dish), smoky barz 126, **127**
chillies 23
    crispy chilli tofu 148, **149**
    fiery chilli pasta 100, **101**
chipotle, jackfruit chipotle burritos 128, **129**
chocolate
    frozen peanut butter & banana bites 200
    obviously chocolatey overnight oats **36**, 37
    one-pan cookie 164
    salted almond butter millionaires 168
    silky chocolate mousse 178, **179**
    soft-baked choc & coffee cookies 166, **167**
    ultimate chocolate smoothie **205**, 206
'chuna' sandwich **72**, 73
ciabattas, creamy harissa chickpea 58, **59**
cinnamon
    beaut berry granola pots 198
    beaut bircher 38
    carrot cake protein balls 203
    cinnamon crunch flapjacks 180, **181**
    elite French toast 183
    fancy apple & cinnamon oven oats 34, **35**
    one-pan cookie 164
    roasted pistachio & pineapple medley 173
    sweet & salty tortilla chips 197
cocoa powder 166, **167**
coconut cream 12
    butter 'chicken' (well actually tofu) curry 120–3
    creamy chickpea curry 112
    Thai-style peanut butter curry 93
    The Salvador Dhali 155
    tomatoey chickpea & broccoli curry 146
coconut (desiccated)
    beaut berry granola pots 198
    blueberry jam 30
    carrot cake protein balls 203
    roasted pistachio & pineapple
      medley 173

coffee
    Mosconi's tiramisu 174
    soft-baked choc & coffee cookies 166, **167**
cookies
    one-pan cookie 164, 165
    soft-baked choc & coffee cookies 166, **167**
courgette
    one-pan breakfast veg medley 51
    one-pot messy veg & rice 102
    pea & mint orzo 145
    Thai-style peanut butter curry 93
couscous, tempeh smash burgers 130
croutons 142, **143**
crumble, miso banana 162, **163**
cucumber
    Bossman's mushroom kebabs 140
    'chuna' sandwich 73
    pickled cucumber 118
    raita, my way 218
    shredded carrot salad 66
    tikka tofu wraps 152
curry 23
    butter 'chicken' (well actually tofu) curry 120–3,
      121–2
    creamy chickpea curry 112, **113**
    Thai-style peanut butter curry 92, 93
    tomatoey chickpea & broccoli curry 146, **147**

D
dates (medjool)
    beaut berry granola pots 198
    carrot cake protein balls 203
    cinnamon crunch flapjacks 180
    salted almond butter millionaires 168
dhal, The Salvador Dhali **154**, 155
dressings 66

E
edamame bean
    Danny Danny noodles 62
    the go-to greens salad 68
    miso greens & gnocchi 138
    miso me up stir-fry 76
    quicker nutty ramen 86
    shredded carrot salad 66
    spiced up fried rice 82
equipment 20

F
fajitas, shredded tofu 70, **71**
flapjacks, cinnamon crunch 180, **181**
flaxseed
    beaut berry granola pots 198
    cinnamon crunch flapjacks 180

fluffy blueberry pancakes 30
tempeh smash burgers 130
French toast, elite **182**, 183

garlicky teriyaki stir-fry 94, **95–7**
gherkin 130–2
glazes 118
gnocchi & miso greens 138, **139**
gochujang 14
granola, beaut berry granola pots 198, **199**
grape & jalapeño salsa **216**, 217
Greek-style yogurt (vegan)
beaut berry granola pots 198
beaut bircher 38
Bossman's mushroom kebabs 140
burger sauce 133
creamy harissa chickpea ciabattas 58
marinade 98
pea & mint orzo 145
raita, my way 218
roasted pistachio & pineapple medley 173
tikka tofu wraps 152

H
hemp seed
blueberry banoffee smoothie 204
get-your-greens-in smoothie 207
obviously chocolatey overnight oats 37
proper porridge with a cherry jam 28
herbs, dried 13
hummus
holy harissa hummus 190, **191**
tomato & butter bean hummus on toast 42, **43**

J
jackfruit
'chuna' sandwich 73
jackfruit chipotle burritos 128, **129**
jalapeño & grape salsa **216**, 217
jam
blueberry jam 30, 31–3
cherry jam 28

K
kale 81
kebabs
Bossman's mushroom kebabs 140, **141**
tofu shish kebabs 98, **99**

lemon
creamy harissa chickpea ciabattas 58
the go-to greens salad 68
holy harissa hummus 190
marinade 98

pea & mint orzo 145
proper peasto pasta 104
sweet & sticky tofu 110
tahini sauce 214
tomato & butter bean hummus on toast 42
lentil(s)
The Salvador Dhali **154**, 155
see also Puy lentil(s)
lettuce 73
lime
boujee black bean & quinoa salad 65
crispy buffalo tofu tacos 156
jackfruit chipotle burritos 128
jalapeño & grape salsa 217
pico de gallo con corn 220
raita, my way 218
spiced up fried rice 82
Thai-style peanut butter curry 93
watermelon sugar shots 184
Lotus Biscoff biscuits, Mosconi's tiramisu 174

M
mac & 'cheese' **136**, 137
mangetout 86
maple syrup 14
marinades 98
meal planners 222–9
millionaires, salted almond butter 168, **169–71**
mint
Green Goddess soup 90
jalapeño & grape salsa 217
pea & mint orzo **144**, 145
proper peasto pasta 104
raita, my way 218
sunny tomato pesto linguine 88, **89**
watermelon sugar shots 184
mirin 14
miso paste 15
miso banana crumble 162, **163**
miso greens & gnocchi 138, **139**
miso me up stir-fry 76, **77**
mousse, silky chocolate 178, **179**
muesli, beaut bircher 38
mushroom
Bossman's mushroom kebabs 140, **141**
Danny Danny noodles 62
miso me up stir-fry 76
one-pan breakfast veg medley 51
one-pot BBQ mushroom rice bowl 60, 61
quicker nutty ramen 86
shredded tofu fajitas 70
tofu shish kebabs 98, **99**
the ultimate quick Bolognese 134

N

noodles
    Danny Danny noodles 62, **63**
    hot boy summer noodles 150, **151**
    miso me up stir-fry 76
    quicker nutty ramen 86, **87**
    simply, a noodle soup 80, 81
nutritional yeast 15
    cherry tomato rigatoni 125
    creamy spinach quesadillas 84, **85**
    fiery chilli pasta 100
    a kind-of carbonara 114
    mac & 'cheese' 137
    Mosconi's tiramisu 174
    the parmigiano alternativo 212, **213**
    proper peasto pasta 104
    ready red pepper pasta 78
    sunny tomato pesto linguine 88, **89**
nut(s)
    beaut berry granola pots 198
    miso banana crumble 162
    quicker nutty ramen 86, **87**
    see also cashew nut; pecan; walnut

O

oat milk
    a kind-of carbonara 114
    mac & 'cheese' 137
    my simple tofu scramble 48
oat(s)
    beaut berry granola pots 198
    beaut bircher 38
    cinnamon crunch flapjacks 180
    fancy apple & cinnamon oven oats 34, **35**
    miso banana crumble 162
    obviously chocolatey overnight oats **36**, 37
    proper porridge with a cherry jam 28
    salted almond butter millionaires 168
olive oil 13
orzo, pea & mint **144**, 145

P

pancakes, fluffy blueberry 30, **31–3**
panko breadcrumbs
    tempeh nuggets 192
    tempeh smash burgers 130
pantry essentials 12–15
parmigiano alternativo, the 212, **213**
passata 120–3
pasta 23
    cherry tomato rigatoni **124**, 125
    fiery chilli pasta 100, **101**
    a kind-of carbonara 114, **115–17**
    mac & 'cheese' **136**, 137

pea & mint orzo **144**, 145
    proper peasto pasta 104, **105**
    ready red pepper pasta 78, **79**
    sunny tomato pesto linguine 88, **89**
    the ultimate quick Bolognese 134, **135**
peanut butter 12
    boujee black bean & quinoa salad 65
    dressings 66
    frozen peanut butter & banana bites 200, **201**
    get-your-greens-in smoothie 207
    quicker nutty ramen 86
    spinach satay side 194
    Thai-style peanut butter curry **92**, 93
pea(s)
    Green Goddess soup 90
    hot boy summer noodles 150
    pea & mint orzo **144**, 145
    peas on toast 39, **40–1**
    proper peasto pasta 104, **105**
    simply, a noodle soup 81
    spiced up fried rice 82
pecan
    beaut bircher 38
    carrot cake protein balls 203
    cinnamon crunch flapjacks 180
    elite French toast 183
    proper porridge with a cherry jam 28
pepper 13
    boujee black bean & quinoa salad 65
    crispy chilli tofu 148
    garlicky teriyaki stir-fry 94
    hearty shakshuka 52
    jalapeño & grape salsa 217
    one-pan breakfast veg medley 51
    one-pot messy veg & rice 102
    ready red pepper pasta 78, **79**
    shredded tofu fajitas 70
    spiced-up fried rice 82
    Thai-style peanut butter curry 93
    tofu shish kebabs 98
pesto, sunny tomato pesto linguine 88, **89**
pick-me-ups 209–21
pico de gallo con corn 220, 221
pistachio, roasted pistachio & pineapple medley **172**, 173
plant milk
    beaut bircher 38
    blueberry banoffee smoothie 204
    fluffy blueberry pancakes 30
    get-your-greens-in smoothie 207
    obviously chocolatey overnight oats 37
    salted almond butter millionaires 168
    ultimate chocolate smoothie 206
    see also oat milk

pomegranate seeds 152
porridge, proper porridge with a cherry jam 28, **29**
potato 90
protein 11
protein powder (vanilla)
    beaut bircher 38
    blueberry banoffee smoothie 204
    carrot cake protein balls 203
    fancy apple & cinnamon oven oats 34
    fluffy blueberry pancakes 30
    frozen peanut butter & banana bites 200
    get-your-greens-in smoothie 207
    obviously chocolatey overnight oats 37
    proper porridge with a cherry jam 28
    ultimate chocolate smoothie 206
puds 159–85
Puy lentil(s)
    one-pot messy veg & rice 102
    the ultimate quick Bolognese 134

Q

quesadillas, creamy spinach 84, **85**
quick eats 55–105
quinoa, boujee black bean & quinoa salad **64**, 65

R

raisin(s) 38
raita, my way 218, **219**
ramen, quicker nutty 86, **87**
raspberry, obviously chocolatey overnight oats 37
rice
    garlicky teriyaki stir-fry 94
    jackfruit chipotle burritos 128
    one-pot BBQ mushroom rice bowl 60, **61**
    one-pot messy veg & rice 102, **103**
    spiced up fried rice 82, **83**
    sweet & sticky tofu 110
    Thai-style peanut butter curry 93
rocket
    boost-me-baby bagel 44
    creamy harissa chickpea ciabattas 58
    tomato & butter bean hummus on toast 42
rose harissa 15
    creamy harissa chickpea ciabattas 58, **59**
    holy harissa hummus 190, **191**
    marinade 98
    tomato & butter bean hummus on toast 42

S

salads
    actually, a decent tomato salad 74, **75**
    boujee black bean & quinoa salad **64**, 65
    the go-to greens salad 68, **69**
    shredded carrot salad 66, **67**

salsa, jalapeño & grape **216**, 217
salt 13
    salted almond butter millionaires 168, **169**
Salvador Dhali, The **154**, 155
sandwiches 23
    'chuna' sandwich **72**, 73
satay, spinach satay side 194, **195**
sauces
    tahini 214, **215**
    teriyaki 94, **95–7**
shakshuka, hearty 52, **53**
smoothies
    blueberry banoffee smoothie 204, **205**
    get-your-greens-in smoothie **205**, 207
    ultimate chocolate smoothie **205**, 206
snacks 187–207
soup 23
    Cal's tomato soup 142, **143**
    Green Goddess soup 90, **91**
    simply, a noodle soup **80**, 81
soy sauce 12
spices 13
spinach
    creamy chickpea curry 112
    creamy spinach quesadillas 84, **85**
    the go-to greens salad 68
    Green Goddess soup 90
    my simple tofu scramble 48
    spinach satay side 194, **195**
    Thai-style peanut butter curry 93
stir-fry
    garlicky teriyaki stir-fry 94, **95–7**
    miso me up stir-fry 76, **77**
strawberry 183
sultana
    beaut bircher 38
    carrot cake protein balls 203
sweetcorn
    pico de gallo con corn 220
    simply, a noodle soup 81

T

tahini 14
    'chuna' sandwich 73
    the go-to greens salad 68
    hearty shakshuka 52
    holy harissa hummus 190
    miso greens & gnocchi 138
    peas on toast 39
    spiced up fried rice 82
    tahini sauce 214, **215**
    tomato & butter bean hummus on toast 42
tempeh
    boost-me-baby bagel 44

hot boy summer noodles 150
a kind-of carbonara 114
tempeh nuggets 192, **193**
tempeh smash burgers 130–3, **131–2**
Tenderstem broccoli
    the go-to greens salad 68
    mac & 'cheese' 137
    miso greens & gnocchi 138
    miso me up stir-fry 76
    simply, a noodle soup 81
    sweet & sticky tofu 110, **111**
    tomatoey chickpea & broccoli curry 146, **147**
teriyaki sauce 94, **95–7**
tikka tofu wraps 152, **153**
tiramisu, Mosconi's 174, **175–7**
toast
    beans on toast 46, **47**
    'chuna' sandwich 73
    elite French toast 183
    hearty shakshuka 52
    my simple tofu scramble 48
    peas on toast 39, **40–1**
    tomato & butter bean hummus on toast 42, **43**
tofu (extra-firm)
    Benny bánh mì 118, **119**
    Bossman's mushroom kebabs 140
    butter 'chicken' (well actually tofu) curry 120–3,
        121–2
    crispy buffalo tofu tacos 156, **157**
    crispy chilli tofu 148, **149**
    garlicky teriyaki stir-fry 94
    my simple tofu scramble 48, **49**
    shredded tofu fajitas 70, **71**
    sweet & sticky tofu 110, **111**
    tikka tofu wraps 152, **153**
    tofu shish kebabs 98, **99**
tofu (silken) 15
    Cal's tomato soup 142
    cherry tomato rigatoni 125
    creamy spinach quesadillas 84
    elite French toast 183
    fiery chilli pasta 100
    hearty shakshuka 52
    a kind-of carbonara 114
    mac & 'cheese' 137
    Mosconi's tiramisu 174
    ready red pepper pasta 78
    silky chocolate mousse 178
tofu (smoked), tofu shish kebabs 98, **99**
tomato
    actually, a decent tomato salad 74, **75**
    boost-me-baby bagel 44
    Cal's tomato soup 142, **143**
    cherry tomato rigatoni **12**4, 125
    'chuna' sandwich 73
    creamy harissa chickpea ciabattas 58
    hearty shakshuka 52
    one-pot messy veg & rice 102
    pico de gallo con corn 220
    posh beans on toast 46
    smoky barz chilli 126
    sunny tomato pesto linguine 88, **89**
    tomato & butter bean hummus on toast 42, **43**
    tomatoey chickpea & broccoli curry 146, **147**
tomato (sun-dried)
    my simple tofu scramble 48
    sunny tomato pesto linguine 88, **89**
tomato paste 13
tortilla wraps
    creamy spinach quesadillas 84, **85**
    crispy buffalo tofu tacos 156, **157**
    jackfruit chipotle burritos 128
    shredded tofu fajitas 70
    sweet & salty tortilla chips **196**, 197

V
vegetables
    one-pan breakfast veg medley **50**, 51
    one-pot messy veg & rice 102, **103**
    pickled vegetables 118
    see also specific vegetables

W
walnut
    carrot cake protein balls 203
    salted almond butter millionaires 168
watermelon sugar shots 184, **185**

Y
yeast see nutritional yeast
yogurt (vegan)
    elite French toast 183
    see also Greek-style yogurt (vegan)

THANK YOUS

As much as I'm personally writing, cooking and testing every single thing in this book, I always say to myself that 'it takes a village' of people to make this happen, and to help me. Before I get into it, I wanna thank you for buying this book, and supporting what I do. Whether you were here from the beginning, from about a year ago, or even found me through this book, you're a bloody legend and I don't any single one of you for granted. We'll go business-y people first and then the family.

I would not be writing this book at this time in my life without the brilliant women at YMU that somehow sensed this in me, but also have helped every step of the way, with both grounding advice and emotional support. Lucy Loveridge, thanks for spotting me on the 'gram, on the telly and thinking 'yeah this bloke is a bit of me, I wanna represent him,' you have genuinely changed my life over the past few years. Lois Sharland, thanks for representing me and managing me through not only this book, but everything else I'm doing in my incredible life. You're driven, can have banter (thank God) and for someone who deals with various talent, you never fail to make me feel included and special with what I'm doing. Anna Dixon, my my, books are your bread and butter. Thank you for introducing me to the wonderful book industry, never saying no to any incredibly audacious ideas I had and really pushing me to make this book into a brilliant piece of work. They'll kick up a fuss if I don't mention their names, but Meghan, Zara, Frankie and Nancy, you're an incredible bunch, and I love coming into the office to both irritate and entertain you. I bloody love you lot.

Next up, Carole Tonkinson. Thanks for taking a punt on me and being the publisher of my first ever book. I am well aware of your successes at Bluebird, and I feel honoured to have been picked up by you lot, especially considering one of my inspirations, Joe Wicks, had the same happen to him years before I came about. The whole Bluebird team, Martha, Mireille, Jodie, Annie, and everyone at Pan Macmillan deserve their thanks, and I will be giving every one of a pat on the back when this book drops. This process has been incredibly eye-opening and hard at times, but throughout it, I felt comfortable, in safe hands and got to work with some incredibly talented people in the industry, all because of Bluebird. It is now, conveniently, my favourite breed of bird. Nic&Lou, thanks for making this book look an absolute stunner, and making it my own, you lot smashed it, and this is all that I could've asked for. Liz and Max, the photographers behind this book and Flossy and Sophie, the absolute dream food stylists. Thank you for making the food look stunning, as well as making me look somewhat decent too. Honestly watching the process come to life has been unreal, and makes me value each and every cookbook out there.

Get the tissues out for this next bit, unless you didn't cry to *Marley and Me*.

Angela, or as I'd call you, mum. You are the biggest motivator for me and I'm genuinely so lucky to know such a kind woman, and all in all, be raised in a way that has shown me what it means to be a good person. You would always clean up after every recipe I tested, always give me feedback both good and bad, and this book is yours, as much as it's mine. You always keep a positive attitude on, you're always there when I need you, both in tough times and fun times, and I do believe it when I tell people that 'I have the best mum in the world.' I love you so much, and I don't care if I come across as a mum's boy.

Lily and Max. Siblings don't usually get on, as I learnt in later life, but somehow, due to sheer luck and me being an absolute babe, you guys are my best friends. I hope you're enjoying the fact that your name is in a proper book. I do always want to say a big thank you for being there to humble me, Lily, you're always the first to tell me if a dish is crap, or if what I'm wearing doesn't work, but I still do it anyway. And thank you for coming up with the title of this book (true story). Max, I wanna say thanks for always bigging me up to everybody you know, except to my face because you know deep down I'll might turn into a cocky bloke. I highly doubt that, but thank you for always supporting me mate.

Dad. I hope you're enjoying the process of watching me turn from a novice who didn't know how to cook and always made the kitchen smell of spices, to a fully published author with banging food. Thanks for giving me the drive to show you can actually do anything you set your mind to, I really do appreciate that.

The Challoner boys. You will be addressed by full name, as some of you are single at the time of writing this. But Mitchell Taylor, Adam Noble, Michael Waight, Andrew Mosconi, Oliver Rowe and Praven Jeyarajah, you lot are my guys. Support networks are highly underrated, and I can't believe we're all still kicking, in touch and loving what life is bringing us all. Thank you for always being there for me and being brilliant mates.

Danny, Hadley, Olivia, you lot are different you know. We're these type of people where you wouldn't see each other for months, and when you do it feels like you only saw them yesterday. That's so rare in life, and I wanna say thanks for making me laugh, smile, letting me be me, and above all, getting me royally drunk on too many occasions to count. Too many

memories, and now it's in print, shame it's not a 3D print for Danny though.

The PLANTBOIIS. Ben, Giuseppe, Johnny, Ebenezer, Jacob, Sam, CJ and Will, we're all in this together, and we've all been there from the beginning of our mad journeys. Thank you all for being sound lads, and not only a pleasure to work with, but absolute diamond geezers and my best mates. I don't know where life's gonna take us all, but I know whatever happens, you all absolutely deserve the successes that are coming. I love all of you.

There's not many people that have been there from the start of my cooking journey, or this social media journey for that matter, but there are two people who have. Liam Charles, baking legend. Thank you for letting me on your Instagram Live back in 2020, and seeing something in this nutter with Jedward hair and thinking 'yeah this geezer is sound.' Your support never went unnoticed and it's a blessing to call you a friend. And Ross Testa. Ross you slid in my DMs (mad innit) and offered your support and guidance as a mentor, and since then, I've been on this mad wave of a career. Thank you for the late-night phone calls, advising me how to run this like a business (which has to be done), and for the endless advice.

I also want to shout out my Instagram mum, dad and sister, Steph, Lewis and Emily, who basically have hyped me up from the beginning and kept it real throughout this mad journey I've had. Love you lot!

And to Héloïse and Belle, thank you for creating the phrase 'bit of me' and basically ruining my vocabulary with this and other terms you SW11 people say.

Carmel, Nathalie, Rich, Jadie, and Mary, aka Nan. I wanna thank the whole of the family I've got, including the fifteen cousins, but you lot are actually so interested in what's going on, and it's so nice to have that unspoken support. I know there's plenty you lot have been doing without me even knowing about, and for that I thank you.

Three 'J's. My last thanks, and yes this is the last one. Joe Wicks. True story, but when I had around about 1,000 followers, I went to one of your runs and you gave me not only advice on how you did it, but you gave me a follow, and kept watching. You never had to do any of the stuff you did, and that you do for others, and I genuinely rate what you've done and will do. Innit bruv. He'll get that, I think. Jamie Oliver. Some of you might know, I went on TV, tried to get a cookbook deal, failed, and still wrote a brilliant one anyways. But I would not have had the expertise, or the knowledge to do so without that show. So Jamie, to you and your team, thanks for providing me a platform to express myself and my food, and for inspiring me and a generation of cooks, that it's okay to do things your own way. And finally, Jamal Edwards MBE. The madness that is life and the madness that was lockdowns, meant we never got to meet in person. But you were the first one, the big player, to big me up, and thousands of other creatives who now smash it in their own fields. If there's one thing I want to thank you for, it's the idea of self-belief you championed. It's genuinely the key to doing whatever you want in life. I send love to you, your family, and your team of people who continue to drive your message and above all, your name will continue to live on. Even through a vegan cook off the internet.

Thank you for making it to the end of this section, and actually the book. No doubt in my mind there's a load of small print at the back, so enjoy that, and I'll see you in the kitchen.

CALUM X

First published 2023 by Bluebird
an imprint of Pan Macmillan
The Smithson, 6 Briset Street, London EC1M 5NR
EU representative: Macmillan Publishers Ireland Ltd, 1st Floor,
The Liffey Trust Centre, 117-126 Sheriff Street Upper,
Dublin 1, D01 YC43
Associated companies throughout the world
www.panmacmillan.com

ISBN 978-1-0350-1365-4

5 7 9 8 6 4

A CIP catalogue record for this book is available from the British Library.

Printed and bound in Great Britain by Bell and Bain Ltd, Glasgow

Publisher: Carole Tonkinson
Editorial Director: Mireille Harper
Managing Editor: Martha Burley
Production Manager: Alenka Oblak
Art Direction and Design: Studio Nic&Lou
Food Styling: Flossy McAslan
Prop Styling: Charlie Phillips